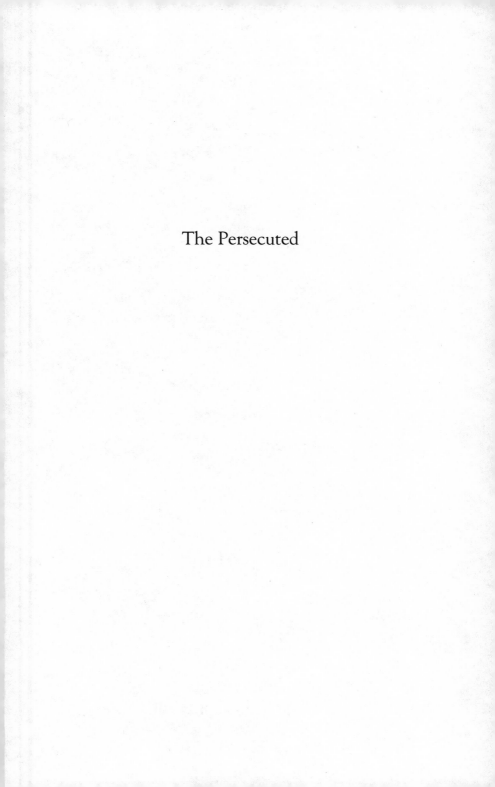

The Persecuted

Casey John Chalk

The Persecuted
True Stories of Courageous Christians
Living Their Faith in Muslim Lands

SOPHIA INSTITUTE PRESS
Manchester, New Hampshire

Sophia Institute Press
Box 5284, Manchester, NH 03108
1-800-888-9344

www.SophiaInstitute.com

Sophia Institute Press® is a registered trademark of Sophia Institute.

paperback ISBN 978-1-64413-550-1

ebook ISBN 978-1-64413-551-8

Library of Congress Control Number: 2021945165

First printing

To all the persecuted Christians throughout the world
whose stories have yet to be told

Truly, truly, I say to you,
unless a grain of wheat
falls into the earth and dies,
it remains alone; but if it dies,
it bears much fruit.

—John 12:24

Contents

Foreword *by Pieter Vree* .ix

Introduction: Asia Bibi and a Trip to Afghanistan 3

1. Encountering the Crisis 11

2. Wilson William and His Family 33

3. Michael D'Souza and His Family 53

4. The Immigration Detention Center 71

5. Heroes and Villains 81

6. Rescuing the D'Souzas from the IDC 93

7. Thousands of Miles Apart 103

8. Rising Fears, Political and Bureaucratic Frustrations . .117

9. Exciting News 131

10. Islamic Extremism Worldwide 141

Conclusion 147

Postscript: Where Do We Go from Here? 157

Acknowledgments 161

Appendix A: Data Substantiating the
Persecution of Wilson William's Family 165

Appendix B: Written Testimony of Ann Buwalda . . .183

Selected Bibliography 199

About the Author 201

Foreword

The persecution of Christians is nothing new. Our Lord Jesus Christ Himself faced persecution, harassment, threats, and stoning attempts throughout His ministry, all before being executed by the reigning Roman government. St. Stephen, whose feast we celebrate the day after Christmas, was the first of many first-century martyrs. For the next three centuries, Roman emperors such as Nero, Domitian, Decius, and Diocletian persecuted Christians wantonly and murdered believers by the thousands, until finally Emperor Constantine signed the Edict of Milan in AD 313, granting complete toleration of Christianity throughout the empire.

But the persecution of the Church isn't merely an ancient Roman tale confined to dusty textbooks. It's alive and well in our world today. Didn't Jesus tell us it would be so? In the Gospel of John, He prepared us for such an eventuality: "If they persecuted me, they will persecute you" (John 15:20). Not only are those who profess faith in Him to expect persecution, but they are also, Jesus told us, to deem it a blessing: "Blessed are you when men revile you and persecute you and utter all kinds of evil against you falsely on my account. Rejoice and be glad, for your reward is great in heaven" (Matt. 5:11–12).

The Persecuted

It should come as no surprise, then, that Pope Francis would say, in April 2016, that persecution is "the daily bread of the Church." During a Mass in Casa Santa Marta, the Holy Father specifically referenced the Pakistanis who lost their lives that year when an Islamic operative of Jamaat-ul-Ahrar, a Taliban splinter group, detonated a suicide bomb in a park in Lahore where Christians were commemorating Christ's Resurrection. "Those Christians who were celebrating Easter in Pakistan were martyred because they were celebrating the Risen Christ," Francis said. "Thus, the history of the Church goes ahead with its martyrs." Or, as Tertullian wrote in the third century, "the blood of martyrs is the seed of the Church."[1]

Unfortunately, the persecution of believers is a reality to which many American Catholics simply can't relate. In our popular culture, persecution impacts ethnic minorities, undocumented immigrants, women, and the transgendered. Christians, even Catholics, are assumed to be thoroughly embedded in the power structure — in other words, part of the problem.

This is ironic because persecution was once a feature of everyday life for Catholic settlers in the United States. Indeed, Harvard historian Arthur Schlesinger Sr. famously called anti-Catholicism "the deepest bias in the history of the American people." However, as historical Protestant prejudices waned, and as many American Catholics heeded the siren songs of secularism, the struggles of our forefathers in the Faith against the Plundering Time, the Know-Nothing Party, the Ku Klux Klan, and the Blaine Amendments became distant, unhappy memories. And immediate environment is a powerful opinion shaper. Christian persecution — does it even exist anymore? It

[1] Tertullian, *Apologeticus* 50, 13.

certainly doesn't fit the dominant American narrative of progress toward world peace.

But persecution is a pesky problem; ignoring it doesn't make it go away. According to the January 15, 2020, annual report from Open Doors USA, a nonprofit organization that tracks religious oppression, 260 million Christians around the globe are facing persecution right now, a 6 percent increase from the previous year. Indeed, "Christians throughout the world continue to risk imprisonment, loss of home and assets, torture, rape, and even death as a result of their faith."[2]

Worse, as the global persecution of Christians has increased, that inconvenient fact is diminishing in importance to American Catholics. A study released in March 2020 by Aid to the Church in Need, an international papal charity, indicated that in 2019, 59 percent of American Catholics said they were "very concerned" about Christian persecution; in 2020, only 52 percent expressed the same level of concern, a drop almost exactly proportionate to the rise in cases of persecution.

One reason for the dip is the dearth of reporting. And so, in my role as editor of the Catholic monthly magazine *New Oxford Review*, I've striven to spotlight the continuing violence and harassment directed against Christians in various parts of the world, especially in the Middle East, where the persecution of men, women, and children who profess faith in Christ Jesus often takes the most extreme and violent forms. But a problem I've consistently faced is that there are few capable Christian writers with firsthand experience with this phenomenon. Often, they must rely for accurate

[2]   Quoted in "Report: Around the World, 260 Million Christians Face Persecution," Catholic News Agency, January 17, 2020, https://www.catholicnewsagency.com/news/43306/report-around-the-world-260-million-christians-face-persecution%C2%A0.

information on wire reports from foreign news agencies or briefs from nonprofit organizations on the ground in far-flung hotspots.

So, when Casey Chalk pitched an article to me in 2016 about his encounters with Michael D'Souza and his family, I jumped at the opportunity to publish it. Here, at last, was an eyewitness account of what the infrequent reports only hinted at. Casey compellingly conveyed the travails of a devout Pakistani Catholic man who had been threatened so severely by local Pakistani Muslim leaders for his refusal to convert to Islam that he had fled, with his family, from their native land for a hand-to-mouth existence on the mean streets of Bangkok. A remarkable angle to the story Casey told—perhaps the most remarkable—was that the D'Souzas, who were struggling to survive in the shadows of Thai society, and then in its prisons, never wavered in their faith in Jesus Christ.

Over the next couple of years, Casey produced five more articles detailing the continuing plight of Michael and his family. In the midst of his reportage, a longtime *New Oxford Review* reader put me in contact with a U.S. congressional representative who, with the help of a nongovernmental organization that tracks the persecution of Pakistani Christians, delivered the D'Souzas' asylum case on the floor of the U.S. Congress.

Alas, the hope we had for the swift resolution of the D'Souzas' resettlement application in the United States was dashed as their case got gummed up in the great gears of government machinery. As an Open Doors report released in July 2020 revealed, there has been a shocking 90 percent reduction over the past five years in the number of Christians resettled in the United States from countries where the Church faces persecution. In 2015, the United States admitted more than eighteen thousand Christians from the fifty countries on Open Doors' 2020 World Watch List for the persecution of Christians, on which Pakistan ranks in the top ten; midway through 2020, the United States had admitted fewer than one thousand.

In addition, there is a terrible temptation for congressional committee members—and indeed, American Catholics—to think of persecution in numerical terms. Two hundred sixty million Christians face persecution? That's almost overwhelming in scope. How many of them can we realistically help? Statistics tend to desensitize, too, as the visceral experience of persecution—the physical, emotional, and spiritual suffering of our fellow believers—fails to register and even death becomes abstract. Numbers, by nature, don't elicit much sympathy.

But this is precisely why Casey's articles, and now this book, are so important: he has put a human face on the suffering that's often hidden behind statistical gloss. We need to hear stories of families like the D'Souzas because we and they are members of the same body, the Body of Christ. Their pain is our pain, their loss our loss, and their joy likewise our joy.

In this book, you will encounter remarkable Pakistani asylum seekers, the D'Souzas and many others. You will be inspired by their immense courage in the face of seemingly insurmountable obstacles; you will sip the bitter cup of institutionalized evil; you will discern the human face of the suffering Church. And you will hearken to the Christian call echoing down the centuries to witness to our Savior with our very lives. In the extraordinary experiences of these exemplary Christian men and women, you will witness, as John Paul II put it, "a living portrayal of Christ's Passion."[3]

—Pieter Vree, *New Oxford Review*

---

[3] "John Paul II's Teaching on the Martyrs of Our Century," Vatican website, https://www.vatican.va/jubilee_2000/magazine/documents/ju_mag_01031997_p-56_en.html.

The Persecuted

Introduction

Asia Bibi and a Trip to Afghanistan

A man's mind plans his way, but the LORD directs his steps.

—Proverbs 16:9

In June 2009, a poor, female Catholic farmhand named Aasiya Noreen Bibi was harvesting falsa berries with a group of poor, female Muslim farmhands in a field in Sheikhupura, Punjab, Pakistan.[4] Bibi lived in the village with her husband and their five children. They were the only Christians in their small community. Some of the Muslim women asked Bibi to fetch water from a nearby well. On her way, Bibi stopped to take a drink using a small metal cup she found next to the well. One of Bibi's neighbors, Musarat, who had been engaged in a feud with Bibi's family over some property damage, observed Bibi's action and

---

[4] Details in this story are primarily taken from Shumaila Jaffery, "Asia Bibi: Pakistan's Notorious Blasphemy Case," *BBC*, February 1, 2019, https://www.bbc.co.uk/news/resources/idt-sh/Asia_Bibi; John L. Allen Jr., *The Global War on Christians: Dispatches from the Front Lines of Anti-Christian Persecution* (New York: Image, 2013), 65–67; and Asia Bibi and Anne-Isabelle Tollet, *Blasphemy, A Memoir: Sentenced to Death Over a Cup of Water* (Chicago: Chicago Review Press, 2013).

declared that it was forbidden for a Christian like her to drink water from the same utensil as a Muslim, and that he and some of the other laborers considered her to be unclean because she was a Christian.

This was not the first time Bibi had been harassed by Muslims in her community. Indeed, she and her family were frequently pressed to convert to Islam. But this event was the tipping point. According to Bibi, when Musarat and others made derogatory statements about Christianity and demanded, once more, that she convert to Islam, she pushed back. "I believe in my religion and in Jesus Christ, who died on the Cross for the sins of mankind," she retorted. "What did your Prophet Muhammad ever do to save mankind? And why should it be me that converts instead of you?" An acrimonious argument ensued.

Then things got violent. An angry Muslim mob appeared at Bibi's home. They beat her, and they beat members of her family. Eventually the police intervened — not to punish the attackers, but, rather, to take Bibi away. An investigation about her remarks was initiated and resulted in her arrest for blasphemy under Section 295 C of the Pakistan Penal Code.

Local police officer Muhammad Ilyas claimed during an interview with CNN that Bibi had said that "the Quran is fake" and that she had made disparaging remarks about the Prophet Muhammad.[5] Village imam Qari Muhammad Salim alleged that Bibi had confessed her blasphemy to him and apologized for her misdeeds, though the Asian Human Rights Commission

---

[5] Reza Sayah and Nasir Habib, "Christian Woman Sentenced to Death for Blasphemy in Pakistan," CNN, November 11, 2010, http://religion.blogs.cnn.com/2010/11/11/christian-woman-sentenced-to-death-for-blasphemy-in-pakistan/.

disputed this allegation and indicated that the village imam had pressed villagers to accuse her of blasphemy and had even used the loudspeakers of the local mosque to spread the allegations of Bibi's supposed crime.[6]

Bibi was imprisoned for over a year before she was formally charged. Finally, in November 2010, a judge at the court of Sheikhupura, Punjab, sentenced her to death by hanging. The verdict, which was reported worldwide, made Bibi the first woman to be condemned to death in Pakistan on blasphemy charges. Bibi later described that day:

> I cried alone, putting my head in my hands. I can no longer bear the sight of people full of hatred, applauding the killing of a poor farm worker. I no longer see them, but I still hear them, the crowd who gave the judge a standing ovation, saying: "Kill her, kill her! Allahu Akbar!"[7]

Ashiq Masih, Bibi's husband, declared his intention to appeal, especially considering court transcripts indicating inconsistencies in evidence presented during the trial. Salmaan Taseer, the governor of Punjab, investigated the case for then-president of Pakistan Asif Ali Zardari and announced the Pakistani president's plans to pardon Bibi. Yet the country's high court, perhaps fearful that clemency would incite countrywide violence, issued a stay order against a potential executive pardon. And indeed, in

---

[6] "Muslim Leaders Who Issued Decree to Kill a Christian Woman Should Be Prosecuted," Asian Human Rights Commission, December 8, 2010, http://www.humanrights.asia/news/urgent-appeals/AHRC-UAC-177-2010/.

[7] Hal St. John, "Ten Million People Now Want to Kill Me," *Catholic Herald* (UK), June 14, 2012, https://catholicherald.co.uk/ten-million-people-now-want-to-kill-me/.

January 2011, Governor Taseer himself was assassinated by his bodyguard for his opposition to the very blasphemy law that had been the cause of Bibi's troubles.

Bibi was placed in solitary confinement in an eight-by-ten-foot cell in a prison in Lahore, one of the country's largest cities. She was kept away from other inmates because other individuals accused of blasphemy had been killed while in Pakistani prisons. Bibi's health deteriorated. She was frequently threatened and physically abused by prison guards.

The Asia Bibi case increasingly drew international attention, from Amnesty International, Human Rights Watch, Voice of the Martyrs, the American Center for Law and Justice, and even Pope Benedict XVI.[8] "People often wonder why and how I became famous around the world," notes Bibi. "They forget that it is thanks to Pope Benedict XVI."[9]

Though condemnation by international leaders and organizations placed pressure on the Pakistani government, it also enraged and provoked Bibi's enemies. Radical religious parties in Pakistan demonstrated in several major cities after the pope's comments. One mullah promised a fifty-thousand-rupee[10] reward to whoever killed Bibi. "I became a symbol for the anti-blasphemy laws," acknowledges Bibi. "When the pope comes

[8] Pope Benedict XVI mentioned Bibi during an address in St. Peter's Square in Rome in late November 2010, declaring: "I am thinking of Asia Bibi and her family, and I ask that she be given her freedom as soon as possible." See Asia Bibi and Anne-Isabelle Tollet, *Free at Last: A Cup of Water, a Death Sentence, and an Inspiring Story of One Woman's Unwavering Faith* (Savage, MN: Broadstreet Publishing, 2020), 61.

[9] Bibi and Tollet, *Free at Last*, 54.

[10] Approximately three hundred U.S. dollars, a not insignificant sum in Pakistan.

to your defense, Islamists see it as a duel between Islam and the Catholic Church."[11]

Bibi's appeal hearings were delayed five times. In October 2014, the Lahore High Court dismissed the appeal and upheld her death sentence. Bibi's husband and her lawyer appealed to the president of Pakistan and to the Pakistani Supreme Court. Four more years of suspensions and delays followed. Finally, on October 8, 2018, eight years after her ordeal had begun, Pakistan's Supreme Court acquitted Bibi of blasphemy charges. The court also censured Bibi's accusers, whom, the justices asserted, "had no regard for the truth."

Bibi was reading the Bible when she heard the news of her acquittal. But various Muslim groups organized widespread protests following the court ruling, which prompted Pakistani authorities to lock down much of the country for days.[12] A vengeful Taliban commando armed with detonators, grenades, an explosive belt, and a map marking Bibi's cell in the prison managed to get inside the building before he was captured by prison guards.[13]

But Bibi's travails were still not over. On November 2, 2018, the government of Pakistan, under the administration of new

---

[11] Bibi and Tollet, *Free at Last*, 65–66. When Salmaan Taseer's assassin, Malik Mumtaz Qadri, was hanged in February 2016, protests erupted across the country, many blaming Qadri's death on Bibi. See Bibi and Tollet, *Free at Last*, 134.

[12] Because of incidents like that suffered by Bibi, the Pakistani Senate's Special Commission on Human Rights, in March 2018, approved a decision to punish severely any accusation of blasphemy that is false or fabricated in order to prevent people from using the blasphemy law indiscriminately. Accusers require two witnesses, but, as Bibi and Tollet note, "finding fake witnesses isn't difficult." See Bibi and Tollet, *Free at Last*, 52.

[13] Bibi and Tollet, *Free at Last*, 123.

prime minister Imran Khan, barred Bibi from leaving the country and subsequently detained her again. This was surprising, as Imran Khan, a former internationally recognized cricket player, had promised to protect persecuted Christians during his campaign. Indeed, following the Supreme Court decision on Bibi's case, Imran Khan had called on Pakistani citizens to respect the rule of law and exhibit restraint.[14]

Once again, international leadership across the Western world—including from Australia, Italy, and Canada—spoke on Bibi's behalf and demanded her release and permission to depart Pakistan. On January 29, 2019, Pakistan's Supreme Court again upheld her earlier acquittal, and once again violent protests erupted across the country.

Some feared that Pakistan, even under the more moderate Imran Khan regime, would never let Bibi leave. But, in fact, there was some logic to Khan's reluctance to release Bibi. "The Pakistani Government was attempting to bide its time so that people would forget about me," explains Bibi. Indeed, prior to the January 2019 verdict, Khan had taken actions to protect Christians and deter the anti-Christian Islamists and ordered the temporary imprisonment of the leader of the Islamist Tehreek-e-Labbaik Pakistan (TLP) party and three hundred of its members.[15] Finally, after another three months, Bibi was quietly flown out of Pakistan. On May 8, 2019, she arrived in Canada, which had graciously agreed to grant her asylum. There she was reunited with her family members who had already fled Pakistan.

When the Asia Bibi blasphemy case began, in 2009, I was preparing for the first of what would become many tours to Pakistan's

14 Bibi and Tollet, *Free at Last*, 148.
15 Bibi and Tollet, *Free at Last*, 162.

next-door neighbor, Afghanistan. Before that trip, my knowledge of South Asia was limited. Yet, much to my surprise, I soon fell in love with Afghanistan and the Afghan people. I developed a strong impulse to learn Dari, the predominant language in much of the country, and I devoured many books on Afghan history and many meals of Afghan cuisine, which seemed to me a harmonious blend of the surrounding Persian, Indian-Pakistani, Central Asian, and even Russian cultures. I also learned that Afghanistan and Pakistan are tightly linked. The 1,500-mile border is quite porous, so, throughout history, people have moved fluidly between the two countries. Indeed, they have often been lumped together under dominions ruled by much greater empires such as the Mongols, the Mughals, and the British. While Pashtuns are Afghanistan's largest ethnic group (nearly 40 percent), there are more than twice as many Pashtuns living in Pakistan, mostly in the provinces along the Afghan border.

My personal and professional interest in Afghanistan thus inevitably led to my studying and learning about Pakistan. Afghanistan's twenty-year-long battle with the Taliban cannot be understood apart from Pakistan, whose remote mountains have provided shelter and defense for Taliban leadership and fighters. Even Osama bin Laden himself lived for years in a walled compound in Abbottabad, Pakistan, only about 160 miles from the Afghan border. To comprehend Afghanistan, one must comprehend Pakistan. To learn Dari, one inevitably learns some Urdu, the predominant language of Pakistan.

But I did not know in 2009, when I first traveled to Kabul, and when Asia Bibi's terrible plight in Pakistan began, that five years later God would find such a different use for my experience in South Asia. I did not realize that my knowledge of the Taliban, my acquisition of Dari, and even my appreciation for spicy South Asian cuisine would help me to champion scores of Christian asylum seekers, so far from both my native United States and their homes in Pakistan. As readers will discover, their stories and experiences are disturbingly similar to Asia Bibi's.[16]

Such is the mysterious work of our Lord. We cannot predict the manifold ways in which He will use our experiences and gifts to build His Kingdom. But we can make ourselves available for that work.

That is one of the most important lessons I have learned over more than ten years of devoting my energies to the people of South Asia. I pray that from this story about Christian persecution, readers will learn an important lesson as well about Christian service and God's grace.

---

[16] See, for example, the case of Christian couple Shagufta Kausar and Shafqat Emmanuel, who, in 2013, were imprisoned and later sentenced to death in Pakistan on charges of sending "blasphemous texts." The two were acquitted in June 2021. See "Pakistan Overturns Christian Couple's Blasphemy Death Sentences," BBC, June 3, 2021, https://www.bbc.com/news/world-asia-57347604.

Encountering the Crisis

Blessed are those who are persecuted for righteousness' sake,
for theirs is the kingdom of heaven.

—Matthew 5:10

"This is the best day of my life!" I had screamed this as I ran around the iconic terrace of the Kennedy Center in Washington, D.C. I was in second grade, and my parents had taken me to a St. Patrick's Day concert by the Chieftains, an Irish music group. On the very same outdoor terrace, twenty years later and again following a Chieftains concert in honor of St. Patrick's Day, I proposed to a beautiful, devoutly Catholic Southern belle. Claire said yes. It would appear God has a sense of humor.

Life moved fast after that exhilarating evening. Barely a month after our engagement, Claire and I resolved to move to Bangkok for my job. But then, shortly after our wedding, we discovered that Claire was pregnant with our honeymoon baby. And then we found out that my father had cancer. Fearing the worst, I backed out of the opportunity in Thailand.

Some months later, in the early morning of April 29, 2013—a Monday—my father, Daniel Francis Chalk, died. The following Thursday, May 2, we held the memorial service at my parents'

Evangelical church. Hundreds came to pay their respects. We were blessed by the turnout but emotionally and spiritually exhausted.

Early the next morning, Claire's water broke.

The next months were hard as I struggled with my father's death, my mother's grief, my wife's recovery, and our new baby girl. But God had a plan. A new professional opportunity presented itself, once more in Thailand. So, in July 2014, we left my mother, our family, and our friends and found ourselves in hot, humid Bangkok. It was a new beginning.

Our downtown twelfth-floor apartment had a breathtaking view of the skyline, and the back porch of the flat overlooked a *klong*, a canal used by locals for their daily urban commute. Within a five-minute walk of our building, a dozen restaurants and a score of street vendors served everything from tourist favorites such as pad thai and pad see ew to Middle Eastern and South Asian dishes such as shawarma and roti. It was overwhelming, intoxicating, and exactly the kind of adventure I had envisioned enjoying with my new bride and our blonde, fair-skinned daughter whom the Thais affectionately labeled *duk-a-dah*—"doll baby."

The closest Catholic parish, Holy Redeemer, was a brisk twenty-five-minute walk from our condo. Half of the Masses at the Redemptorist-run parish were in English and half in Thai. All the priests were Thais, with the exception of an ancient missionary from Kansas who had moved to Thailand in the 1950s.[17]

To Westerners, Holy Redeemer seems to have a peculiar architectural style, as it resembles the ubiquitous Buddhist *wats*, or

[17] I discovered later that this priest had celebrated the marriage of my boss and his wife at the same parish about twenty years earlier. My boss told me that, during the initial interview, the priest, in his rural Kansan accent, had asked the bride-to-be if she had ever "been a man." Such is Thailand!

temples, found across the city. Indeed, on the church's altar stand several bulb-shaped furnishings that symbolize royalty in Thai culture. But the idea was endorsed by Venerable Fulton Sheen, who reasoned that the Catholic Church should accommodate itself to the art and architecture of host cultures, as long as there was no compromise on doctrine.

The congregation at Sunday Mass was the most diverse I had ever witnessed. Of course, there were many Thais. But there were almost as many Western expatriates, largely from the United States, the United Kingdom, and Australia, as well as a sizable Filipino community and a good number of West Africans. Yet the most intriguing people I observed that first Sunday at Holy Redeemer were the South Asians. Based on their dress and my knowledge of the region, I suspected they were Pakistanis.

On our second Sunday at Holy Redeemer, I approached one of the greeters, a youthful-looking South Asian man who was handing out church bulletins, and asked him where he was from. "Pakistan," he answered. "Karachi." I told him I knew that city was a great metropolis as well as an extremely dangerous, lawless place, where gangs operated with impunity. He was incredulous that I knew *anything* about his hometown.

The man's name was Wilson William. I didn't know then that he would become one of my best friends in Bangkok.

I told Wilson I had visited Afghanistan many times, that I knew a little Dari and Urdu, and that I had some familiarity with the current political situation in Pakistan, including the persecution of Christian communities.[18] He told me that was precisely why he and his family were in Bangkok.

---

[18] I had also gained familiarity with the persecution of Christians in Pakistan from my days as a Protestant seminary student.

The Persecuted

After Mass, Wilson introduced me to his extended family: sixteen people, including his elderly parents and several young children from multiple families. He told me that many of the other South Asians at Holy Redeemer were there for similar reasons, as were the hundreds, if not thousands, of other Pakistani Christians across the city. The vast majority of them were asylum seekers fleeing religious persecution and awaiting processing by the United Nations High Commissioner for Refugees, or UNHCR.

The UNHCR would study each case, conduct an interview, and then determine whether an asylum seeker's grievances were formally sufficient to justify refugee designation, thereby extending the legal protections that status entails—as well as the potential opportunity to settle in a country that accepted refugees, such as the United States, Canada, or the United Kingdom. The process typically took years. But as I would discover in time, it usually did not have a happy ending for the Pakistanis. Even if the refugee designation was approved, *less than 1 percent* of all globally U.N.-designated refugees are placed in another country every year.[19]

So it was that in the late summer of 2014, on a Sunday at Holy Redeemer Church, my family's relationship with the Pakistani asylum-seeker and refugee community in Bangkok began. Their heart-wrenching but inspiring stories merged with my family's story. The testimony of these brave Catholics would profoundly impact our lives, as well as the lives of many of my close family and friends.

One of my professors, Patrick Sookhdeo, had written a book on the subject: *A People Betrayed: The Impact of Islamization on the Christian Community in Pakistan* (Pewsey, Wiltshire, U.K.: Isaac Publishing, 2002).

[19] UNHCR, Resettlement Data, January–May 2021, UNHCR, https://www.unhcr.org/en-us/resettlement-data.html.

Before I share Wilson's story, it is important to understand the context and origin of the humanitarian crisis in Pakistan. For the situation in Pakistan is, in many ways, a microcosm of the experience of Christians throughout the Islamic world. When you understand what Christians experience daily in the region, you will appreciate why millions of Christians—not only in Pakistan but across the Muslim world—feel compelled to flee their homes and put themselves at the mercy of a foreign country in an alien culture.

As Middle Eastern Christians are proud to note, Christianity predates Islam in the region by a good six hundred years. From its birthplace in ancient Palestine, Christianity quickly spread into the valley of the Indus River, which runs north to south across present-day Pakistan. According to Christians in the southern Indian state of Kerala, the Christian faith first reached the Indian subcontinent in the first century AD, brought by the apostle Thomas. By the sixth century, its adherents were governed by Assyrian Christian bishops from Persia.[20]

The Arab and Muslim military leader Muhammad bin Qasim conquered the province of Sindh in the early eighth century, facilitating the spread of Islam across the subcontinent. A succession of Muslim empires (the Ghaznavid Empire, the Ghurid Kingdom, the Delhi Sultanate, the Mughal Empire) would dominate the western and northern regions of the subcontinent for the next thousand years, ensuring the dominance of the Islamic religion in what would become Pakistan.

In the seventeenth century, Portuguese Jesuits, Augustinians, and Carmelites penetrated several areas of present-day Pakistan,

---

[20] Sookhdeo, *A People Betrayed*, 39.

including Lahore, Karachi, and Kashmir, though their missionary efforts did not win a significant number of converts.

The British conquest of Sindh in 1842 markedly changed things for those in the western part of the subcontinent. More Catholic missionaries moved into Hyderabad, Karachi, Lahore, and Sialkot and built schools, orphanages, and churches. These missionary activities reaped significant dividends in the first decades of the twentieth century. Between 1901 and 1931, the Catholic population of Punjab increased from 1,500 to 45,641. There were similar explosions in conversions to other Christian denominations, including the Presbyterians, Anglicans, Salvation Army, Methodists, and Baptists.

Though originally part of the British Raj (when the British Empire governed India), Pakistan became an independent nation following the 1947 partition of the Indian subcontinent between Hindu-dominated India (led by Hindu nationalist Mohandas Gandhi), and Muslim-dominated Pakistan (led by Muslim nationalist Muhammad Ali Jinnah).[21] In this new nation, only about four hundred thousand people, less than 1.5 percent of the population, were Christians.[22]

For the first few decades following Pakistani independence, the Christian population continued to expand. The number of Catholics in the country almost tripled to more than three hundred thousand, many of whom were converts from Protestant

[21] John L. Esposito, *Islam: The Straight Path*, 4th ed. (New York: Oxford University Press, 2011), 165–168; Owen Bennett Jones, *Pakistan: Eye of the Storm*, 3rd ed. (New Haven: Yale University Press, 2009), 43–52.

[22] Sookhdeo, *A People Betrayed*, 58–62.

denominations.[23] There were, however, some troubling signs. The constituent assembly formed to guide Pakistan through its first years of self-rule and independence from Britain included no Christians, even though there were nineteen non-Muslims out of a total of seventy-two members.

Yet, as was so often the case during the postcolonial era, this (ostensibly) secular nationalist movement proved fertile breeding-ground for Islamism. As the influence of Western empires declined, religious extremism rushed in to fill the void.

So, following Jinnah's death in 1948, efforts intensified among Muslim groups to make Pakistan into an Islamist state. Marginalization of the Christian community intensified under the presidency of General Zia-ul-Haq (1977–1988), even while the Christian population increased to somewhere between 1.3 to 3 million people.[24] Zia seized power from Zulfikar Ali Bhutto in a 1977 coup and promoted Nizam-e-Mustafa, or Islamic sharia law, by seeking to radicalize the country's constitution in favor of Islam. Modifications to the constitution, for example, implied that minority communities, including Christians, were not full and equal citizens of Pakistan.[25]

General Zia's promotion of the Hudood Ordinances, which sought to implement Sharia law and bring Pakistani law into "conformity with the injunctions of Islam," did much the same. His administration also encouraged the broadening of the country's blasphemy laws, which restricted and punished perceived criticisms of Islam.

As in the rest of the Muslim world at the time, various political groups advocated for Sharia, especially for the Sharia teaching

[23] Sookhdeo, *A People Betrayed*, 53.
[24] Sookhdeo, *A People Betrayed*, 68.
[25] Sookhdeo, *A People Betrayed*, 99–116.

that non-Muslims are *dhimmi*, a protected but inferior class of people. Religion scholar Patrick Sookhdeo explains:

> Each step towards greater enforcement of the Sharia brings as an automatic "by-product" a lessening in status of non-Muslims. This may not always involve practical changes in the law, but will at the very least take place simply by reinforcing in the mind of Pakistani Muslims the place of the Sharia in their faith, including its teaching on the rights and status of dhimmi in comparison with the rights and status of Muslims.... The Sharia creates a mindset of anti-Christian discrimination which individuals may put into practice with greater or lesser attention to the limits set out in the Sharia.[26]

Here, too, Pakistan proves an excellent case study. The more Sharia took precedence in legal proceedings over the articles and clauses in the country's (secular) constitutions and laws, the more threatened the country's Christian population became. Unsurprisingly, discrimination against Christians rose significantly following Zia's administration. Indeed, writing in 1999, investigative journalists Cathy Scott-Clark and Adrian Levy claimed that Pakistani Christians had effectively become "worse off than the untouchables of India," because they were socially stigmatized for being both poor and Christian.[27]

Under Islam, the Hindu caste distinctions were, in theory, abolished. But marginalization of lower castes, so deeply rooted in the subcontinent's culture, nevertheless persisted. Many

[26] Sookhdeo, *A People Betrayed*, 184, 238.
[27] Cathy Scott-Clark and Adrian Levy, "Beyond Belief," *Sunday Times Magazine*, January 24, 1999.

Christian converts were drawn from this underclass, exacerbating the discrimination and stigmatization they face today, not only in Pakistan but in virtually every Muslim-majority country in the world.

In the late twentieth century, Islamist sentiment continued to grow throughout the region. New and even more brutal restrictions were placed on religious minorities, especially Christians.

For example, in 1982, an amendment to Pakistan's Penal Code, Section 295-B, made the willful defiling or damaging of a copy of the Quran an offense punishable with mandatory life imprisonment. Four years later, another amendment, Section 295-C, made it a crime to insult the Prophet Muhammad, regardless of whether the insult was done deliberately or with criminal intent.[28] These additions have become convenient weapons for settling personal disputes between Muslims and non-Muslims.

These "blasphemy laws" which, in the West, were abolished hundreds of years earlier—are still common in the Islamic world. To this day, they are also a weapon that aggrieved Muslims use to punish those who cause perceived religious offenses.[29] The blasphemy legislation has become a constant source of fear for the Christian community, aggravated, notes Sookhdeo, by a number of factors:

> The method of investigation of complaints, which is biased in favor of the accuser; the Islamic tradition of confounding blasphemy with the capital crime of apostasy; the Islamic tradition of private individuals enforcing death sentences for crimes against Islam; the influence of

[28] Sookhdeo, *A People Betrayed*, 250–251.
[29] Sookhdeo, *A People Betrayed*, 301.

local mullahs in rousing popular sentiment against alleged blasphemers.[30]

The tenuous rule of law in many such nations also makes charges of blasphemy inherently political, both in courts and, even more so, in the court of national public opinion, which has become increasingly zealous in maintaining religious purity. Indeed, many powerful "conservative" parties are explicitly and aggressively Muslim in character.

In Pakistan, for example, the Muslim League (not surprisingly) made its appeal to Muslims in the February 1997 elections with the slogan "If you are a Muslim then join the Muslim League." Another Islamic party, Jamaat-e-Islami, ran on the slogan "What is the meaning of Pakistan? There is no God but Allah and Muhammad is His Apostle!"[31]

The first case to be registered under Pakistan's new blasphemy laws was that of Daniel Scot, a Christian teaching at the Government Degree College in Okara. Two professors at the college filed a case against Scot in September 1986, accusing him of insulting the Prophet Muhammad. The two academics also incited a mob of five thousand students, many armed with guns and knives, against Scot. The Christian teacher went into hiding. In October 1986, more than one hundred Christian leaders petitioned General Zia on Scot's behalf. But Scot and his family eventually fled to Australia.[32]

The first Christian to be convicted under the blasphemy laws was Gul Pervaid Masih, who lived in a village in north-central Pakistan. In 1991, members of his village paid him to repair a

[30] Sookhdeo, *A People Betrayed*, 302.
[31] Sookhdeo, *A People Betrayed*, 347.
[32] Sookhdeo, *A People Betrayed*, 257–260.

communal water tap, which he did. When it failed again later that year, one of Masih's neighbors, Sajjad Hussein, who was allegedly a member of a militant Sunni group, accused Masih of pocketing the repair money. A heated argument ensued, and a witness of that argument filed a First Information Report, or FIR, to a local police station. Masih and his brother were arrested on charges of making derogatory remarks about the Prophet Muhammad and one of Muhammad's wives, Aisha.[33]

Although the police deemed the brothers innocent, no lawyers could be found to represent them at their trial. Despite the fact that only one individual (Hussein) spoke against Masih, the sessions judge declared him guilty and sentenced him to death *and* a five thousand rupees fine. The judge asserted that the accuser, Hussein, possessed the "beard and outlook of being a true Muslim" (yes, the judge explicitly commented on his beard), and thus, he had no reason to doubt his testimony. Masih appealed the death sentence and was acquitted by the Lahore High Court in November 1994. Soon thereafter, he fled to Europe.[34]

Nor were these new laws a dead letter. Over the next decade, convictions under these new blasphemy laws increased during the 1990s.

Hence the case of Tahir Iqbal, a retired Pakistani Air Force mechanic who was paralyzed in his lower limbs. He was accused

---

[33] Aisha was also an authoritative source of Muslim teaching. According to the ninth-century hadith Sahih al-Bukhari, 7:62:64, Aisha was nine years old when her marriage to Muhammad was consummated. See also Andrew Rippin, *Muslims: Their Religious Beliefs and Practices*, 3rd ed. (New York: Routledge, 2005), 297, and Farid Esack, *The Qur'an: A User's Guide* (Oxford: Oneworld Publications, 2005), 39.

[34] Sookhdeo, *A People Betrayed*, 260–263.

of blasphemy, arrested, and imprisoned. He died in July 1992 while in custody. Naimat Ahmer, a Christian schoolteacher, was stabbed to death in January 1992 following an accusation of blasphemy. Bantu Masih, another Christian, was murdered by his accuser in May 1991 while in police custody. Manzoor Masih, yet another, was shot and killed when he left the Lahore High Court on bail in April 1994.

Often, Pakistani police appear powerless to stop this religiously motivated persecution—and sometimes they explicitly support it. Sookhdeo explains:

> The police commonly not only turn a blind eye to crimes against Christians but also very often exhibit the same prejudices themselves. Hence the frequent reports from Christians about visiting the police station to report a crime of which they were the victim and finding themselves beaten up by the police.[35]

In Pakistan, this was evidenced in early February 1997, when thousands of Muslims, egged on by clerics at local mosques, attacked Christians in the villages of Shanti Nagar and Tibba Colony in Punjab Province, while the local police did nothing. Almost eight hundred houses were looted and set on fire, while much of the communities' infrastructure was damaged or destroyed. Several Christian women and girls in the villages were kidnapped during the riots, which ended when the Pakistani army eventually intervened.[36]

Perhaps one of the most dramatic signs of Christian pessimism in the face of rising Muslim antipathy toward them was

[35] Sookhdeo, A People Betrayed, 356.
[36] Sookhdeo, A People Betrayed, 264–275.

the shocking May 1998 suicide of Rev. John Joseph, Catholic bishop of Faisalabad (and the first indigenous Catholic bishop). The bishop — who was a fairly polarizing figure because of his willingness to confront Muslim extremism in Pakistan aggressively — committed suicide to protest the execution of another Christian falsely accused of blasphemy.[37] His suicide note expressed the bishop's hope that his death would be the first "sacrifice" in a reinvigorated campaign to repeal the blasphemy law.[38]

The increased radicalization of the Muslim world appeared to reach new heights in the early 2000s. No single event in recent history had a more significant impact on this marginalized community than September 11, 2001.

Al-Qaeda, headed by the infamous Osama bin Laden, had been given asylum in Afghanistan by the Taliban, the brutal Islamic extremist movement that had ruled the country since 1996.[39] The locus of the United States' military retaliation after the 9/11 attacks was centered squarely on Afghanistan, so bin Laden and a few al-Qaeda operatives fled into the mountains of Pakistan. The mastermind of 9/11 eventually set up residence in a nondescript compound in Abbottabad, in the western part of the country.[40]

---

[37] Mathew Schmalz, "Remembering Bishop John Joseph of Pakistan," *Crux*, May 6, 2015, https://cruxnow.com/church/2015/05/remembering-bishop-john-joseph-of-pakistan/.

[38] Sookhdeo, *A People Betrayed*, 318, 349.

[39] Ahmed Rashid, *Taliban: Militant Islam, Oil and Fundamentalism in Central Asia*, 2nd ed. (New Haven: Yale University Press, 2010).

[40] Lawrence Wright, *The Looming Tower: Al-Qaeda and the Road to 9/11* (New York: Vintage Books, 2007), 402–421.

The Persecuted

Though many Afghans cheered the U.S. military assault on the Taliban, many Muslims in Pakistan perceived the West's incursion into their backyard less warmly. "Christians in Pakistan were subjected to retaliation from Muslims seeking vengeance on supposed allies of the Americans," observes Sookhdeo.[41]

The U.S.–led coalition deposed the Taliban regime and formed a democratic government in Kabul. But although the Taliban were beaten, they were not broken. Many fighters fled into Pakistan's mountainous western provinces, a region dominated by Pashtuns (the same ethnicity as most Taliban members) who shared similar conservative Muslim beliefs.[42] Indeed, a madrassa, or Islamic religious school, founded by Pakistani religious and political leader Sami-ul-Haq, had been a major training ground for the Taliban's leadership.[43] The Taliban had established a robust network of *shuras*, or councils, across western Pakistan. The primary goal of this network was to sponsor a resurgent Taliban insurgency — one that would, in several years, come to control more than a third of the country.[44]

---

[41] Sookhdeo, *A People Betrayed*, 352.

[42] Steve Coll, *Ghost Wars: The Secret History of the CIA, Afghanistan, and Bin Laden, from the Soviet Invasion to September 10, 2001* (New York: Penguin Books, 2004), 62.

[43] The Taliban practice an extremist form of the conservative Deobandi tradition of Islam, a movement that began in nineteenth-century India but developed significant strongholds in Pakistan after the country attained independence in 1947. See Rashid, *Taliban*, 88–90. Rashid notes that, in 1999, at least eight cabinet ministers of the Taliban government in Afghanistan were graduates of Sami ul-Haq's extremist Deobandi seminary in the North-West Frontier Province of Pakistan.

[44] Rashid, *Taliban*, 227.

The Taliban's extremist ideology also inevitably spread among Pakistan's own Muslim populations, given the long-shared cultural and linguistic history among Pashtuns. By 2007, militant groups in the same remote regions (known as the North-West Frontier Province and the Federally Administered Tribal Areas) who had engaged in sporadic revolt against the Pakistani government had coalesced into the Pakistani Taliban, or Tehrik-e-Taliban Pakistan (TTP). Like the Afghan Taliban, it was dominated by Pashtuns and maintained the same rigid form of Islamic belief and practice.[45]

To combat the Taliban's increasingly effective insurgency against the nascent Afghan government, U.S.-led military efforts began focusing their attention on the border areas of northwest Pakistan that harbored Taliban insurgents. This, in turn, led many Taliban and al-Qaeda fighters to flee their mountain havens in favor of more populated parts of Pakistan, including Karachi, a city of almost fifteen million people. Meanwhile, hundreds of thousands of displaced refugees from those same provinces migrated to Karachi because of Pakistani military operations aimed at combating Taliban-aligned insurgencies.[46]

News media in 2009 and 2010 began reporting speculations that then-Taliban supreme leader Mullah Omar had shifted his base from Quetta, near the Afghan border, to Karachi. In a period of just a few weeks in late 2009, Karachi police arrested more than 450 illegal foreign residents, mostly Afghan and Uzbek citizens suspected of having ties to militants.[47] When the *Washington Post*, in

[45] Rashid, *Taliban*, 239.
[46] Imtiaz Ali, "Is Karachi Becoming a Taliban Safe Haven?," Institute for Social Policy and Understanding (ISPU), January 1, 2010, https://www.ispu.org/is-karachi-becoming-a-taliban-safe-haven/.
[47] Ali, "Is Karachi Becoming a Taliban Safe Haven?"

2014, asked a senior Karachi police commander about the number of Taliban sympathizers living in the city, he bluntly estimated "a couple hundred thousand." The same article cited Pakistani officials and analysts who estimated that the number of active militants who were members of either the Taliban or similar Muslim extremist groups was between ten thousand and fifteen thousand.[48]

Again, while the American invasion of Afghanistan has certainly had the most direct impact on Pakistan's Christian population, other conflicts in which the U.S. military has been involved, such as Iraq, Libya, Syria, and Yemen, have also had an effect. These nations are understood to be part of the "land of Islam" (Dar-al-Islam) by many Muslims. Western military activities there are thus perceived by many Muslims, and certainly those adhering to its more conservative manifestations found across Pakistan, as a direct affront to the Islamic world. Islam scholar John L. Esposito explains:

> Anti-Americanism is driven not only by the blind hatred of terrorists, but also by a broader based anger and frustration with American foreign policy among many in Arab and Muslim societies: government officials, diplomats, the military, businessmen, professionals, intellectuals, and journalists.[49]

Each news report of Western military operations in Dar-al-Islam, therefore, reinforces already strong anti-Western sentiment

---

[48] Tim Craig, "Karachi Residents Live in Fear as Pakistani Taliban Gains Strength," *Washington Post*, February 14, 2014, https://www.washingtonpost.com/world/karachi-in-fear-as-pakistan-taliban-gains/2014/02/03/010aafea-8991-11e3-833c-33098f9e5267_story.html.

[49] Esposito, *Islam*, 241.

among many Muslims, which has consequences for their Christian neighbors. As Sookhdeo explains: "This attitude can manifest itself in anti-Christian action, following the age-old equating of the Western world with the Christian world."[50]

☛ Pakistan's Christians certainly were not spared this backlash. In August 2002, gunmen threw grenades into a chapel in northern Punjab, killing four and wounding twenty-five. In September 2002, Muslim gunmen murdered six people at a Christian charity in Karachi. In December 2002, following an Islamic cleric's call for Muslims to kill Christians, two burqa-clad Muslim gunmen threw a grenade into a Presbyterian church in eastern Pakistan, killing three girls. In November 2005, three thousand militant Islamists attacked Christians in Sangla Hill in Pakistan and destroyed Roman Catholic, Salvation Army, and United Presbyterian churches.[51]

Violence became even more intense and high-profile in the second decade of the twenty-first century. In March 2011, Shahbaz Bhatti, federal minister for minorities affairs in the Pakistani government, and a Catholic, was assassinated by gunmen for his opposition to Pakistan's blasphemy laws.[52] In September 2013, 75 Christians at the Anglican All Saints Church in Peshawar were killed by an extremist suicide attack.[53] Attacks on two churches in Lahore on March 15, 2015, killed 15 Christians and wounded

---

[50] Sookhdeo, *A People Betrayed*, 237.

[51] Allen, *Global War*, 85–87.

[52] Allen, *Global War*, 90–91.

[53] Ismail Khan and Salman Masood, "Suicide Attack at Christian Church in Pakistan Kills Dozens," *New York Times*, September 22, 2013, https://www.nytimes.com/2013/09/23/world/asia/pakistan-church-bombing.html?_r=0.

70.[54] On Easter Sunday, March 27, 2016, a suicide bomber affiliated with the Pakistani Taliban attacked Christians at a playground in Lahore, killing at least 70 and wounding more than 340.[55] On December 17, 2017, a bomb attack on a Methodist church killed 9 and injured 57.[56]

These anecdotes and statistics, when cited in aggregate, can both overwhelm and desensitize. Nevertheless, it's important to realize how anti-Christian riots, kidnappings, bombings, murders, theft, and destruction of property have become common experiences for Pakistani Christians.

Can it be any surprise, when the culture of Pakistan is so arrayed against Christians? According to Asia Bibi, the famed survivor of Pakistan's blasphemy laws:

> Even though we are not considered a threat, we aren't respected either.... We have to state our religion on our identification papers, and our passport has a different color: black. Before anyone opens it, they already know we are Christians. It's as if we have a mark in the middle of our faces, and in Pakistan, this mark is not an asset. The vast

[54] "Worshippers Killed in Pakistan Church Bombings," Al Jazeera, March 15, 2015, https://www.aljazeera.com/news/2015/3/15/worshippers-killed-in-pakistan-church-bombings.

[55] Annie Gowen and Shaiq Hussain, "Death Toll in Pakistan Bombing Climbs Past 70," *Washington Post*, March 28, 2016, https://www.washingtonpost.com/world/death-toll-in-pakistan-easter-suicide-attack-rises-to-72-authorities-vow-to-hunt-down-perpetrators/2016/03/28/037a2e18-f46a-11e5-958d-d038dac6e718_story.html.

[56] Syed Ali Shah, "9 Killed in Suicide Attack on Quetta's Bethel Memorial Methodist Church," *Dawn*, December 17, 2017, https://www.dawn.com/news/1377184.

majority of Christians are limited to cleaning the streets, and we are called *choori*, an extremely demeaning, even insulting, nickname that basically means "a person who cleans the toilets." In the countryside, it is difficult for us to own land because Muslims refuse to sell their seeds to us at a reasonable price.[57]

Almost twenty years ago, Sookhdeo observed that "Christians feel increasingly that they have no place in Pakistan and are unsure whether their identity as Christians is compatible with being Pakistanis."[58] How much more does that statement ring true now, when hundreds of Christians have been murdered because of their faith and dozens of churches have been destroyed.

Another terrifying trend is the prevalence of the abduction, rape, and forced marriage of Christian girls to their rapists. Abducted Christian girls are forced to convert to Islam, which makes their coerced marriages legal under Sharia-influenced legal codes. Some of these girls are as young as twelve years old.[59] Most of them are from poor families who lack the power or resources to resist. According to the Movement for Solidarity and Peace, a Pakistan-based human rights organization, approximately one

---

[57] See Bibi and Tollet, *Free at Last*, 46.

[58] Sookhdeo, *A People Betrayed*, 347.

[59] For example, in December 2020, twelve-year-old Pakistani Christian Komal Gulzar was raped during an attempted kidnapping in the Sheikhupura district of the Punjab province. See Kamran Chaudry, "Uproar Over Rape of Christian Women in Pakistan," *Union of Catholic Asian News*, January 11, 2021, https://www.ucanews.com/news/uproar-over-rape-of-christian-women-in-pakistan/90954.

thousand Christian and Hindu women and girls are abducted every year in Pakistan.[60]

A 2017 article in the *National Catholic Reporter* noted one such case in Pakistan, in which a married Christian mother in her twenties was abducted and forced to marry her Muslim abductor. When her Christian husband reported this crime to the police, they refused to do anything because the Christian marriage was not registered under Pakistani law. After the woman escaped, her new Muslim "husband" went to the police. The authorities took his side over the Christian husband because the Islamic marriage was legally registered.[61]

On April 28, 2020, a Christian girl named Maria Shahbaz was kidnapped by three armed Muslim men close to her home in Madina Town, near Faisalabad. She was subsequently coerced into a marriage to one of the men, Muhammad Naqash. Shahbaz's mother, Nighat, in May 2020 told reporters, "I beg that my daughter be returned to us. I am frightened that I will never see her again."[62] A lower court then intervened and placed Maria in a women's shelter, pending further investigation. However, on August 4, 2020, the High Court in Lahore — despite being supplied by Maria's parents with a birth certificate demonstrating

[60] Ashfaq Yusufzai, "Minorities in Pakistan Fear 'Forced Conversion' to Islam," Inter Press Service, May 19, 2014, http://www.ipsnews.net/2014/05/minorities-pakistan-fear-forced-conversion-islam/.

[61] Thomas Reese, "Pakistani Christians Abducted, Raped and Forced into Marriage," *National Catholic Reporter*, July 13, 2017, https://www.ncronline.org/blogs/faith-and-justice/pakistani-christians-abducted-raped-and-forced-marriage.

[62] Mike Thomson, "Abducted, Shackled and Forced to Marry at 12," BBC, March 10, 2021, https://www.bbc.com/news/stories-56337182.

that she was underage—ruled that Maria was legally married to Naqash and that she was required to be "a good wife" to the man.[63]

For anyone familiar with the Islamic world's recent history, the cases of Asia Bibi, Maria Shahbaz, and Wilson are not anomalies. They are symptomatic of what has become the cruel norm for Christian minorities not only in Pakistan but across "the land of Islam." They suffer countless injustices and are desperate for help.

---

[63] Barnabus Fund, "Pakistani Court Returns Kidnapped Christian Girl, 14, to Muslim Man Who Forced Her into Marriage," August 5, 2020, https://news.barnabasfund.org/Pakistani-court-returns-kidnapped-Christian-girl--14--to-Muslim-man-who-forced-her-into-marriage/.

2

Wilson William and His Family

For God alone my soul waits in silence;
from him comes my salvation.
He only is my rock and my salvation,
my fortress; I shall not be greatly moved.

Psalm 62:1–2

Wilson's story begins with his brother, Younas, a Catholic physician who lived and worked in Karachi, Pakistan. In March 2011, several Muslim mullahs approached Younas and forced a Quran into his hands. The Quran contained ripped pages, which were conveniently visible when they shoved it into his hands. The men quickly took pictures of the confused Younas holding the Quran. The mullahs then began claiming that Younas had disrespected the Quran. They told him the pictures would be used as evidence against him in a blasphemy charge.[64]

---

[64] Such allegations are not infrequent. In late December 2020, three young Pakistani Christians were arrested on allegations they had burned pages of the Quran near the homes of Muslims. See Libby Giesbrecht, "3 Pakistani Christians Charged with Blasphemy," CHVN Radio, January 10, 2021, https://chvnradio. com/articles/3-pakistani-christians-charged-with-blasphemy.

Members of the local Christian community, including Younas's father and brother, arrived at the scene and were able to free Younas from the mullahs. The Muslim clerics, however, warned that they would come back with the police. Not long thereafter, vans of Karachi police and Pakistan Rangers, a paramilitary law-enforcement body, arrived at Wilson and Younas's home to apprehend them.

The family immediately left their house and ran to their local Catholic parish, St. Jude, again with help from members of their community. Their parish priest, Fr. Richard D'Souza, was able to save them from arrest by speaking with the local authorities.

That very same day, the family determined it was in their best interests to leave their Christian community in Pahar Ganj, their neighborhood in Karachi. Following the advice of Fr. D'Souza and a local NGO, the National Commission for Justice and Peace, Younas and his wife and children fled to another Christian community in Karachi called, appropriately, Christian Town.[65] Meanwhile, news of the Quran incident involving Younas began to appear in local media, including on the television program Samaa News and in the Karachi-based newspaper *Janbaz*.[66] Rumors began circulating that mullahs were holding meetings to discuss Younas's alleged blasphemies and their intention to find Younas and burn him alive for revenge.

---

[65] See appendix A for a copy of a letter written by the NCJP describing the persecution of Wilson's family.

[66] See appendix A for an image of the newspaper clipping. The relevant excerpt from the Urdu-language Pakistan newspaper *Janbaz* reads: "In the area of Pahar Ganj, a Pakistani organization and the Christian community had tension due to a Christian man named Younas Masih who disrespected the holy Quran and tore the papers of the book."

A Christian police officer named Tariq Mashi had helped Wilson's extended family leave their Christian community for Christian Town. Mashi's daughter had been kidnapped and gone missing.[67] On April 29, 2011, reporters from German and French news channels visited Wilson's family, conducted interviews, and videotaped the family in their new home. The reporters also interviewed Fr. Richard from St. Jude, members of the local NGO, and Tariq Mashi.

In the weeks that followed, the family heard rumors that mullahs were continuing to organize meetings against the family and to plot their deaths. Their revenge would be a "lesson" to all Pakistani Christians.

Fearful for their lives, the family moved once more, to Essa Nagri, another Christian neighborhood in Karachi. These constant moves were an additional, frustrating hardship. Besides Wilson's and Younas's immediate families, the extended family comprised more than a dozen people, including their aging mother and father, their widowed sister, Catherine, and her three children, Sania, Sunil, and Sameer, and Sania's husband, Bulbul. It was difficult to avoid being noticed while moving quickly in and out of neighborhoods.

Wilson began receiving ominous calls demanding that he provide his brother's address and threatening to kill his family in revenge for their alleged disrespect of the Quran. When Wilson told his parish priest about the phone calls, his priest advised him to change his mobile phone number. These threats also dissuaded many extended members of the family from visiting them.

Younas, meanwhile, was shepherded out of the country with his wife and three children to Thailand, where they eventually

[67] As of the publication of this book, Mashi's daughter is still missing.

obtained refugee status. The family was subsequently offered asylum in the Netherlands, where they now live. But despite all of this, Wilson and his family did not want to leave Pakistan. Rather, they tried to start a new life in a rented house in Essa Nagri.

About a year later, on August 6, 2012, Wilson's wife, Nasreen Maryam, was working a shift as a nurse at the Ziauddin Hospital in Karachi. A Muslim patient accused Maryam of dishonoring Islamic prohibitions during Ramadan when she gave him an injection that resulted in his breaking his Ramadan fast. The patient also alleged that Maryam had prayed for him to be a Christian. Maryam's supervisor at the hospital called Wilson and urged him to come to the hospital immediately.

Wilson went to the hospital with his sister Catherine and his other sister's husband, Shamim Gill. When they arrived, Maryam was wailing loudly and declaring that she was innocent and had given the injection to the Muslim patient only after receiving orders from a Muslim doctor. She told Wilson that the patient and the doctor seemed to be attempting to entrap her. The supervisor, Saima, asked Maryam to write down her side of the story, which she did. Then Saima urged them to leave via a back door in the rear of the hospital.

As they were leaving in a taxi, the son of the Muslim patient spied Wilson, Maryam, and their relatives. He ran toward them, firing a handgun. The four, terrified, hid their heads in their knees. The taxi driver, thinking a thief was firing at them, sped away quickly. By God's grace, Wilson asserted, the family was able to reach their home in Essa Nagri safely. There were bullet holes in the roof of the taxi.

When Maryam told the story to their extended family, they wept and wondered why trouble seemed to haunt their family, whose members so desperately wanted to be left alone to live, work, and worship in peace. When Maryam called her supervisor, Saima, and told her about the man shooting at them, Saima urged them to call the police and give them a written statement of the incident. But she also told Maryam not to return for her work shifts at the hospital until further notice.

The family then contacted their parish priest, Fr. Richard. He told them that he would send someone to collect all the information on the incident. Khokhar M. Saad, who worked for the NGO World Human Rights, arrived at their home, recorded their story, and then went to the hospital to gather further information.

A little while later, Saad contacted Wilson and advised him that Maryam should not return to the hospital. A blasphemy charge via a police First Information Report, or FIR, had been registered against her. (FIRs can often be procured via bribes, as corruption in Pakistani police departments is systemic.) Even more distressed, Wilson and Maryam were unable to sleep. Wilson was afraid to tell his parents about the FIR because his father had a heart condition and his mother was a diabetic with hypertension.

The next morning, Maryam's supervisor called and told her that she should not return to duty because of the FIR. Saima added that the police had taken a file from the HR department that included her home address. Saima urged Maryam and Wilson to turn off their phones and move to another place because authorities would soon be arriving with an arrest warrant.[68]

Maryam was crying in fear and said she wanted to go speak with Fr. Richard. She and Wilson disguised themselves and went to the parish. The priest told them that he already knew

---

[68] See appendix A for court documents regarding the blasphemy allegations against Maryam.

everything about their situation, including the FIR, and that authorities were already looking for her in the neighborhood of their previous residence, Pahar Ganj. Fr. Richard recommended that if Wilson and Maryam felt safe in Essa Nagri, they should not go out in public—including visiting the church—until things had calmed down. He urged them to call him if they had any problems and told them that he would talk to the NGO on their behalf.

On August 26, 2012, Wilson's seventeen-year-old niece, Sania Salamat, was going to church when a Muslim mullah stopped her and asked if she was a relative of Nasreen Maryam. She admitted that she was. He began forcibly pulling her arm and declaring that her whole family had disrespected the Holy Prophet Muhammad and that they were all worthy of death. He also claimed that Younas had disrespected the Quran and cowardly fled Pakistan to avoid punishment.

He began dragging Sania away, telling her that he would convert her to Islam and force her to marry another mullah. But providentially for Sania, the mullah was alone and Wilson's sister Catherine, with the help of her son Sameer and some other nearby members of their community, were able to free Sania. The man ran away, threatening that he would come back with his friend and take Sania.[69] Unfortunately, from that time on, Wilson and Maryam's neighbors all knew that their family was the one whom mullahs were actively and prominently seeking.

---

[69] See appendix A for a copy of the newspaper clipping. An excerpt from the Urdu-language Pakistan newspaper *Qumirala* reported on the incident: "Sania Salamat, while on her way to church, was approached by a mullah who tried to kidnap her and rape her but due to the crowd he was not able to do so."

Shortly thereafter, against the advice of Fr. Richard, they visited their old parish. Fr. Richard told them that he had heard that their names had been placed on the wall of a local mosque for disrespecting Islam. During that visit, they also learned that an unnamed Muslim had issued a fatwa against them. The fatwa asserted that whoever killed even one person of their family would go directly to Heaven.[70] Upon hearing this, the family was struck with grief and, amid many tears, prayed to God for mercy.

Afterward, the NGO employee Khokhar Saad urged Fr. Richard to move Wilson's family to another place, lest other members of the church or community become targets of the mullahs. Saad asked Wilson if he had any relatives who could help, but Wilson told him that all his relatives had stopped talking to them out of fear of Muslim reprisals. Saad put the family in a van and took them to a Christian town where Wilson's sister-in-law lived.

There they stayed for three months, "like prisoners," as Wilson later described it. The family was prohibited from going outside. While they were there, Wilson's older sister Parveen, who still lived in their old neighborhood of Essa Nagri, called Wilson's sister-in-law in tears and told her that mullahs, accompanied by local police and Rangers, had come to Essa Nagri looking to arrest Wilson's family. Parveen's mother-in-law grabbed the phone

[70] See appendix A for a copy of the fatwa. The fatwa was issued by Mufti Haji Sheikh Amin Ahmed, at the Jamia Masjid al Muqaddas Mosque in Karachi. It read that the Mufti "has issued this as a death penalty against Nasreen Maryam and against her family members named William Masih, Wilson William, Gulzar William, Catherine Salamat, and Sania Salamat for disrespecting the holy Quran, tearing and burning the holy papers from the Quran. Therefore this whole family has done a sin against Islam, so this family is eligible to die, and anyone who finds this pagan family and kills them will go directly to heaven."

from her and said that it would be a great kindness to them if Wilson's family never contacted them again. She did not want to end up in the same kind of trouble Wilson and Maryam now found themselves in. She added that the day after the original incident with Maryam, representatives from a local Pakistani news station had come and interviewed them.

In September 2012, taking the advice of Fr. Richard, the family registered for passports to leave Pakistan.[71] Meanwhile, everyone with whom they communicated urged them not to share any information about them with Pakistani authorities if the family was apprehended and questioned. All their friends and family were terrified of being associated with Wilson's family, as they, too, might become targets of Muslim extremists.

On the morning of December 21, 2012, Saad came with another man and gave Wilson newspaper clippings that reported on the incidents involving Wilson's family—a concerning though important development, as it provided impartial proof of the family's persecution that would prove useful to them when they applied for refugee status. Even more positively, Saad told Wilson that the NGO had arranged for an evening flight to Thailand and that he would return to take them to the airport. That night, thirteen members of Wilson's family—Wilson, his wife and three children, his mother and father, his widowed sister and her three children, and his niece and her husband—boarded an airplane destined for Bangkok, where they arrived on December 22, 2012.

Only four days after Wilson's family arrived in Thailand, mullahs set fire to the home of one of Wilson's older sisters, Nasreen

---

[71] See appendix A for a letter from Fr. Richard D'Souza describing the persecution experienced by Wilson's family.

Laiquat. Nasreen and her two daughters, Sonam and Urshia, were severely burned.[72] Fearful of further violence, Nasreen called Wilson in Thailand and told him she wanted to hand over custody of her two daughters to Wilson and his elderly father.

Fortunately, Sonam and Urshia, as well as Nasreen's son Urshaman, were eventually able to flee Pakistan. They arrived in Bangkok in March 2014. Nasreen herself remained in Pakistan. About six months later, her phone was disconnected, and Wilson has not heard from her since. To this day, he does not know whether Nasreen is alive or dead.

In April, another family friend, Naomi Patras, also made it to Bangkok. Naomi's uncle had been a close friend of Wilson in Pakistan. Naomi, a teacher in the city of Sargodha in northern Pakistan, had been accused by some students' parents, as well as some school administrators, of applying discriminatory practices toward non-Muslims in her classroom. Without a job, and fearful of retaliation, she fled Pakistan.

Thus, by the spring of 2014, Wilson, who would celebrate his thirtieth birthday in May, had become the *de facto* head of a sixteen-member asylum-seeking family in Pakistan.

⌒

After my initial encounter with Wilson at Holy Redeemer in the late summer of 2014, he and I soon became friends. It became our usual custom to chat for a few minutes before Sunday Mass and for our children to play together afterward. Wilson would tell me about his family and their well-being. His parents, William Masih and Gulzar Bibi, were in deteriorating health, both

---

[72] I saw the burn marks on the torsos of Sonam and Urshia during my time in Thailand.

showing early signs of either dementia or Alzheimer's. His father was also partially deaf.

He would also update me on his refugee application. Not long after arriving in Bangkok, Wilson had applied to the UNHCR for formal refugee status in the hopes of being resettled to another country—perhaps Holland, where his brother Younas lived. In the months that passed, they relied on their own meager savings and doing odd jobs for parishioners to make ends meet. Wilson's niece Sania Salamat gave birth to a baby who died shortly after birth. That put her into a state of shock that led her to avoid coming out in public, even at Holy Redeemer.

The family provided copies of all their documentation to the Thai parish priest at Holy Redeemer, Fr. Phaiboon, who spoke with Fr. Salhedago, one of the priests in Karachi who was familiar with their story. Moreover, the Karachi Catholic bishop, Joseph Coutts, who was later named a cardinal by Pope Francis, visited Bangkok in March 2014 and also told Fr. Phaiboon about their situation.[73]

Only a few months after I met Wilson, he informed me that another priest friend of theirs, Fr. Thomas, was arriving from Karachi. Claire and I were excited to meet him, and we invited Wilson and Fr. Thomas to dinner at our condo. When I came to collect Fr. Thomas and Wilson in the late afternoon, the brisk, twenty-five-minute walk proved too much for Fr. Thomas, who was in his sixties and in poor health, compounded by a foot problem that inhibited his range of motion. So I hailed three motorcycle taxis, and Wilson and I helped Fr. Thomas onto one of them. As the

[73] See appendix A for a copy of a letter from Archbishop Coutts to the UNHCR in Bangkok regarding Wilson's family's situation, as well as a letter by Fr. Phaiboon describing the same.

motorcycle drivers bobbed and weaved through the traffic, I kept anxiously turning around to make sure Wilson and Fr. Thomas were still behind me.

When we pulled up at my building, I was in a sweat only partially caused by the Bangkok heat. I fumbled for cash and handed over what I thought was a 100 Thai baht bill, about three U.S. dollars—a fair price for three motorbike taxis driving a mile. The lead driver quickly grabbed the money and sped off. Wilson grabbed my arm and shouted, "Do you realize you just gave that driver a 1000 Thai baht bill!" That was still only a little over thirty U.S. dollars. But Wilson, who usually ate meals that cost the equivalent of a dollar or less, must have thought my wife and I were millionaires. All I could do was shrug it off to my own *farang* (Thai for "foreigner") ignorance.

The security guards at my building must have been curious as I walked into the lobby with Wilson and Fr. Thomas. Many in downtown Bangkok are familiar with the large, illegal asylum-seeker population. Of course, Fr. Thomas had a valid tourist visa. But Wilson did not. The best thing to do was to act confident. As we went up to the twelfth floor in the elevator, I wondered what Wilson, who lived so humbly in Thailand, would think of our spacious three-bedroom condo, paid for in full by my employer.

I was grateful that Claire's Southern hospitality was in full force. Dinner was prepared; the table was beautifully set. Fr. Thomas accepted a Thai beer; Wilson declined. Alcoholism is a problem for Pakistani asylum seekers in Thailand, where alcohol is cheap and Pakistanis are understandably depressed and vulnerable.

Fr. Thomas turned out to be a world traveler, having visited much of the English-speaking world to attend various Catholic conferences and events. He even served as an adviser for a number of English-language liturgical initiatives around the globe. He told us about the difficulties his parish in Karachi frequently encountered. Local Muslims constantly complained about his church and its "noise"—the ringing of bells, the playing of music, the use of speakers to amplify homilies out into the church courtyard. These complaints did not fall on deaf ears with local police, who, probably out of a combination of fear of Muslim extremists and sympathy with their conservative preaching, often came to the parish and demanded that the Christian worshippers be quiet.

Moreover, said Fr. Thomas, while the persecution of Wilson's family was certainly an extreme example of the animosity and violence faced by Pakistani Christians, it was by no means atypical. Many of Fr. Thomas's parishioners had been harassed, attacked, or, in the case of some young women, kidnapped and forcibly married to Muslim men. It was obvious that Fr. Thomas, a well-educated man with much professional experience, was infuriated by the persecutions his flock was suffering at the hands of a rising number of ignorant extremists in Karachi.

After dinner, Fr. Thomas quite unexpectedly took out an aspergillum, a liturgical implement used to sprinkle holy water. He declared he would bless our house. We did not tell him that another priest friend of ours, a Marist missionary from New Zealand, had blessed our home only a few weeks earlier. We were grateful to have the blessings of a man who seemed to me practically a living saint. Claire took a picture of Fr. Thomas, Wilson, and me, and I escorted them outside, praying that God would get them safely home without interference from nosy taxi drivers or suspicious Thai police officers.

Fr. Thomas left for Pakistan a few days later. It was obvious that his visit had been an encouragement to Wilson's extended family, though in other ways it only reinvigorated their feelings of frustration with their predicament. About a year later, Wilson told me after Mass that Fr. Thomas had died back in Karachi. I wondered: Were there many Pakistani Catholics eager to enter seminaries to replace men like Fr. Thomas?[74]

☙

On March 27, Easter Sunday, 2016, terrorists linked to the Pakistani Taliban launched a suicide attack on picnicking families in the city of Lahore, a Pakistani metropolis with approximately 11 million people. The attack killed more than 70 people and wounded 230 others, many of whom were Christian women and children. I read the news on Easter Monday shortly before departing to lector at Holy Redeemer in Bangkok.[75]

During Mass, as the priest prayed the Collect, I glanced beyond the threshold of the open-air church and saw a funeral procession honoring a recently deceased Thai parishioner. Two Pakistani teenage pallbearers were solemnly carrying her coffin to an awaiting hearse. I knew the Lahore news must be on their minds too.

That Pakistanis would solemnly serve in a Thai funeral at an English-speaking parish spoke powerfully to the universality of Christ's Church. It was a remarkable testimony to how Christians, through their suffering, can fulfill St. Paul's words in Colossians 1:24: "In my flesh I complete what is lacking in Christ's afflictions for the sake of his body, that is, the church."

[74] See appendix A for a copy of a letter written by Fr. Thomas regarding the persecution of Wilson's family.

[75] Many of the details in this section can be found in Casey Chalk, "Murdered Christian in Lahore, Vulnerable Christians in Bangkok," *Ethika Politika*, April 1, 2016, https://ethikapolitika. org/2016/04/01/the-response-to-lahore-resides-in-bangkok.

The Persecuted

The pallbearers in question were members of Wilson's extended family. Since they had arrived in 2012 and 2014, they had lived in two tiny one-room apartments a stone's throw from the Catholic parish. Having visited their humble home many times, I knew they were packed in like sardines at night, sleeping on the floor on thick mats. Since their arrival in Thailand, they had become the parish's "utility infielders," doing any odd job required by the church: handing out bulletins, helping with the collection, setting up chairs before weddings and funerals, and cleaning up afterward.

Wilson's family defied the usual description of asylum seekers and refugees as poor, weak, and helpless persons entirely dependent on the beneficence of Western donors. Rather, these were a hardy, hardscrabble bunch, with an independent, indefatigable work ethic. At the beginning of Lent, Wilson had told me that he and his family would be performing the same fasts done by Muslims during Ramadan (no eating or drinking from dawn to dusk). When I remarked (with obvious admiration) on it, Wilson and his family responded: "Well, we are asking for a lot."

Because of their diligence and holiness, they had won many friends and supporters at Holy Redeemer. This was quite a task in a parish that supports literally thousands of asylum seekers from Pakistan and elsewhere. Indeed, when Thai authorities would do periodic roundups of asylum seekers who had overstayed their visas, a parishioner who was a Thai national with local police connections would give them an early warning so they could lie low for a few days.

But after more than a year of waiting, Wilson's family was informed that their refugee applications to the UNHCR had all been rejected. According to the official UNHCR paperwork, the rejection was because of a "lack of credibility and inability to provide sufficient details" and "unclear and vague statements."

Wilson was particularly frustrated with the UNHCR's description of his father, whose interview, the documentation claimed, lacked clarity and was full of discrepancies. "He can't even remember what he had for breakfast this morning; how is he supposed to remember things that happened years ago in Pakistan?" Wilson asked me in exasperation.

Wilson also claimed the UNHCR-provided Urdu interpreter was a Muslim who was unsympathetic to their cause and who lied to the UN about the specifics of their case. Others familiar with the growing refugee crisis in Bangkok say it is also common for asylum seekers to use someone else's story when offering their testimony before the UN: If a different Christian's story of persecution is more compelling, why not try that one instead? It's possible another asylum-seeker family had stolen Wilson's story and that the interpreter or UN officials were less sympathetic to the family.

The family's last option was to appeal the UNHCR ruling. The appeal, conducted through the Asylum Access, an NGO that helps asylum seekers in Bangkok, noted Wilson's concerns with the Muslim interpreter as well as his father's memory loss. Wilson's appeal, in its conclusion, read as follows:

From 2009 to the present my family has been persecuted by Muslim mullahs in Pakistan, who are still looking for us. We lived in a Muslim society where value and respect are only given to Muslims. We cannot go back to Pakistan, because we know people are looking to attack us and kill us. We have much proof of this with the fatwa, the FIR, and the burning of my family members, who are with us in Thailand and can present evidence of their scars from the attack. There is no life for us in

Pakistan, and we must find a new life somewhere else. We beg you to please take pity on us and examine our case with a gracious heart and make a decision that will allow my family to live a peaceful and free life according to our faith, and where we can find dignified work again to care for our family.

The appeal process, which is allowed only once, takes months or even years. The UN is notoriously understaffed and under-funded in Bangkok. So Wilson's family waited once more, stubbornly faithful and hoping that their story would eventually be told enough times for somebody to save them from the interminable purgatory of indecision and ambiguity. They were understandably angry—both with the bureaucracy and with the West, which had so readily accepted the Muslim refugees who, to quote Wilson and his family members, are "troublemakers."

Of course, the reality is more complicated. Many Muslim asylum seekers fleeing violence in Afghanistan, Libya, and Syria share more in common with my Christian friends than with the terrorists responsible for high-profile attacks that occurred around the same time, such as those in Paris and Brussels.[76] Yet the point still stands: for all the political rhetoric about prioritizing persecuted minority Christians, what exactly were governments doing to save those communities? After all, while the suffering of

[76] I refer to the November 13–14, 2015, ISIS-perpetrated terrorist attack in Paris that killed 130 people and wounded 494 and the March 22, 2016, terrorist attack in Brussels that killed 32 people and wounded 90. For more information, see "2015 Paris Terror Attacks Fast Facts," CNN, November 13, 2019, https://www.cnn.com/2015/12/08/europe/2015-paris-terror-attacks-fast-facts/index.html and "Victims of the Brussels Attacks," BBC, April 15, 2016, https://www.bbc.com/news/world-europe-35880119.

Muslims should not be diminished, Christian minority populations across the Muslim world—such as Wilson's family—are in a categorically different position: they are increasingly unwelcome in their ancestral homes.

Several months after Wilson's family submitted their appeal, I fortuitously encountered a UNHCR officer at my favorite burger joint in Bangkok. I demanded answers, admittedly a bit abruptly. The UNHCR official calmly and graciously explained his own dilemmas and said he would try to help, but I could tell he was in over his head. There are no easy answers to the asylum-seeker problem in Bangkok. And the Thai authorities whom Western media have demonized for terrorizing the asylum-seeker population deserve credit. For all their transgressions, which are many, there is a reason why the persecuted Church is fleeing to Thailand. It is a place where they have a decent chance of being left alone.[77]

༜

During the last week of Advent 2016, a beautiful, seven-week-old baby girl was baptized in Holy Redeemer Church in Bangkok.

---

[77] A U.S. Department of State official who at one time worked with UNHCR in Bangkok told me that UNHCR, as an unannounced matter of policy, will refuse to grant status to large groups if doing so would create a "pull factor." They are no doubt aware that every Christian (along with a very large number of others) in Pakistan could meet the legal definition of a refugee. If they did Refugee Status Determinations, or RSDs, in a technical, "by the book" manner, half of Pakistan would buy a ticket to Bangkok tomorrow—the millions of persecuted and millions more who don't especially enjoy living in Pakistan. The Thai government would, of course, be unable to turn its customary blind eye.

The Persecuted

It was no ordinary Baptism.[78] This little girl—who remained miraculously tranquil during the proceedings—as well as her parents were Pakistani Catholics. The baby was the first child of Wilson's nephew Bulbul and his wife. The Baptism was a manifestation of the true meaning of Christmas.

• Bulbul did not fit the common stereotypes of a third-world refugee. With a bodybuilder's stature and a handsome physique, he exuded the poise of a Bollywood film protagonist rather than someone cowering in fear of his persecutors. If jihadists ever challenged him to a fair fight, he would kick their teeth in. But his physique notwithstanding, the true source of his family's strength—like that of Mary and Joseph, who stood in assured defiance of worldly powers—was their faith and their faithfulness to Christ.

To baptize this infant girl publicly, with Thai police officers only blocks away, was a confident, rebellious act of Christian piety. "You cannot have our bodies or our souls," it proclaimed to those seeking to snuff out the Gospel. This little girl, they asserted with saintly swagger, was claimed for Christ. Pulsing with the Holy Spirit and clothed in righteousness, she carried more spiritual power within her than all the authorities of the earth. The baby was, in her own little way, "a light for revelation to the Gentiles" (see Luke 2:32).

Not that the circumstances of such a Christmas would be desired by anyone else. Jesus' parents probably did not want to go to Bethlehem. They certainly would have preferred not to flee Herod for an unknown Egypt. Likewise with my Pakistani

---

[78] Many of the details in this section can be found in Casey Chalk, "A Christmas Baptism in Exile," *The Catholic Thing*, December 27, 2016, https://www.thecatholicthing.org/2016/12/27/a-christmas-baptism-in-exile/.

friends. Yet here they were, by the grace of God. What made their experience so spiritually potent was their indelible faith that God was with them, that He would not abandon them, and that He was accomplishing His purpose amid what seemed the worst of circumstances.

⌒

In our years in Bangkok, Wilson's family became some of our closest friends.[79] Nevertheless, cross-cultural communication was never easy. Wilson's English was good enough for social conversation. But when we got to specific details regarding his refugee application, it became harder to understand all the intricate details. There were also socioeconomic barriers: What should a middle-class American talk about with poor, marginalized asylum seekers from impoverished Pakistan? "You spent your week avoiding Thai authorities, looking for menial jobs, and eating the same rice and noodles every day? Wonderful! I went wherever I pleased, spent an evening working on my backhand slice, and drank beer at a sky bar."

All the same, we entered into the very heart of their lives. We shared smiles, news of family members, jokes about our priest's homilies. Our children often played together after church. Wilson's family routinely prepared food for me to take home and share with the rest of my family; it was so spicy I was often the only one who would eat it. Before Mass, Wilson's two nephews, both altar servers, always made sure that the celebrating priest

---

[79] Many of the details in this section can be found in Casey Chalk, "Jesus in Thailand: The Christian Asylum Seekers of Bangkok," *Touchstone* (May/June 2018), https://www.touchstonemag.com/archives/article.php?id=31-03-018-c.

reserved a small cup of the Precious Blood for my wife. She has celiac disease and needs to drink from the chalice, rather than receiving the Host, to avoid consuming too much gluten. In Thailand, the disease is practically unheard of, and many Thais, including some priests, scoffed at what they perceived to be an attempt by a Westerner to get special treatment. But Wilson's family never scoffed.

I do not think Wilson was eager to tell other asylum seekers at Holy Redeemer about our friendship, but it was impossible to hide it. And there were a *lot* of Pakistani asylum seekers in need. Many times, as I left the church after weekday Mass, usually in a hurry to make a meeting at work, asylum seekers would approach me to beg for money. Often the request would come with a heartbreaking story I simply did not have time to hear. At other times, the stories bordered on the humorous.

Once, an Ethiopian Orthodox man approached me on the street to tell me his story—one marked by adventure, loss, and poverty. He concluded by telling me: "You've been to Ethiopia. You know our faith in Christ. You know people from my country don't lie." I considered whether an entire nationality could have achieved perfect fidelity to the eighth commandment.

Yet there were a few other asylum-seeker families besides Wilson's with whom we became intimate. Michael D'Souza, whose story is no less dramatic or horrifying than Wilson's, was one such person. Like Wilson, Michael would permanently affect our family's experience in Thailand.

3

Michael D'Souza and His Family

How long will you set upon a man
to shatter him, all of you,
like a leaning wall, a tottering fence?
They only plan to thrust him down from his eminence.
They take pleasure in falsehood.
They bless with their mouths,
but inwardly they curse.
For God alone my soul waits in silence,
for my hope is from him.

—Psalm 62:3–5

If you had come to Bangkok between late 2012 and fall 2016 and visited the Redemptorist parish located there, arriving either before or after Mass, you would likely have seen a Pakistani man, about forty years old, kneeling very conspicuously a few steps below the altar, a rosary prominently raised above his head, held forth as an offering to God.[80] In his other hand would have been a breviary with a worn cover and countless prayer cards jutting

---

[80] Many of the details in this section can be found in Casey Chalk, "A Witness in Bangkok: An Anniversary in Exile," *New Oxford Review* 83, no. 10 (December 2016).

out from between the faded pages, and on it the man's attention would have been rapturously fixed. You would have heard his voice, audible even from the very rear of this large church as he uttered not only Rosaries but innumerable other recognizable intercessory formulas, a profusion of petitions suggesting a deep familiarity with the art of supplication. The man's prayers testified to his faith in the faithfulness of God, his hope that He is listening amid the relentless persecution of Christian populations across the globe. His name was Michael, and when I met him, he was an asylum seeker living in Thailand.

Michael is half South Asian, his mother's family having hailed from Goa, a state on the southwest coast of India known for its Christian population and Portuguese cultural influence; indeed, it was a Portuguese colony for about 450 years. His father's family is Portuguese; his father, Cajetan, moved to Pakistan after marrying Michael's mother. Michael grew up in Karachi, where Cajetan finally purchased a home in the Mahmudabad neighborhood of the city in the early 1990s, when Michael was a teenager.

Around the same time, Michael began working at the Karachi Grammar School, an Anglican-affiliated institution. In January 2001, he married Rosemary Schroeder, the daughter of a Pakistani woman and a German sailor who, like Michael's father, had emigrated to Pakistan. Eighteen months after the wedding, in September 2002, the intimations of future persecution began: Muslim hard-liners who disapproved of Michael's public brand of piety persuaded the school's leadership not to renew his contract.

In May 2003, Michael acquired a position with American Express Travel. When his father died two and a half years later, in October 2005, Michael hosted various family members and neighbors for the wake at his home in a predominantly Christian neighborhood. Two mullahs, Muhammad Danish and Muhammad Nasir, arrived at Michael's home, claiming to be members of the Tehrik-e-Taliban Pakistan, or TTP, an Islamic extremist group and cousin of the more infamous Afghan Taliban known for its antipathy to Christians. They told Michael they were sorry for the loss of his father and that Allah would bless Cajetan in Heaven.

In January 2006, the same two men returned to Michael's house with four or five other young men. The group was going door-to-door in the neighborhood, preaching to the head of each Christian family and ominously inviting them to learn about the Quran and the prophet Muhammad and to accept Islam. They preached at Michael's home for about fifteen minutes before leaving. This became a regular event, occurring four more times that year and five times in 2007. Different people came each time, though Michael still remembers many of their names: not only Danish and Nasir, but also Mullah Nazar Muhammad Naqshbandi and Muhammad Shafiq Khan. During a February 2007 visit, Mullahs Danish and Nasir told Michael that he would be "safe" if he accepted Islam. Michael responded that he respected Islam but politely refused the offer of conversion. "I don't know about Islam," Michael declared. "I know about Jesus." At this, the men began to speak to one another in Pashto, and then one of the young men brandished a gun and threatened Michael. He warned: "It is better for you to study Islam and we will come again soon." Michael told them that would not be necessary, as they were not welcome to return for another visit.

In January 2008, Michael quit his job with American Express. He had been mugged and threatened at gunpoint by a Taliban motorcyclist. Six months later, in July, he and his family were traveling from their house to St. Anthony Catholic

Church, about four kilometers away, when they were ambushed by several Muslim men, including Mullahs Danish and Nasir. The mullahs and their mob followed them all the way to St. Anthony, yelling abusive language and ridiculing the Christian faith. They called Michael a *kafir*, a derogatory Arabic word meaning "infidel" and often used by Muslims to refer to Christians. This continued after Michael and his family departed the church and became a somewhat regular occurrence when they went to worship.

After half a year of unemployment, Michael persuaded the pastor at St. Anthony, which was run by Franciscans, to hire him as a sacristan. In May 2009, Mullah Nasir, Mullah Nazer Muhammad, and Mullah Nazar Muhammad Naqshbandi discovered that Michael was working at St. Anthony. They stopped him outside the church and told him that they knew he was avoiding them. They told him that he did not understand Islam and that they planned to change that, whether Michael liked it or not. Mullah Nasir mocked Christianity, slapped Michael, threatened him, and warned that this harassment would continue. True to his word, five TTP members ambushed Michael and Rosemary in November 2009 while they were walking home from St. Anthony. The men hit Michael on the mouth so hard that he began to bleed and then punched him in the stomach. When he bent down in pain, they kicked him. Afterward, Michael and his family refused to leave their house for several days. Rosemary told a neighbor about what happened. The neighbor suggested that the D'Souzas move to another house.

Again, in March 2010, several of the same mullahs stopped Michael under the same bridge near St. Anthony Church. They physically assaulted and verbally abused him and exhorted him to stop going to church. They threatened to kidnap his wife and daughter and forcibly convert them to Islam. On April 10, 2010, Michael quit his job as sacristan because of the mullahs' threats. Yet this did not stop the harassment. In June 2010, Mullahs Danish and Nasir came to his house again. When Michael refused to let them in, they stood at the gate shouting, declaring that the households that the mullahs visit must convert or they would be killed.

In September 2010, Mullahs Danish, Nasir, and Naqshbandi and several others stopped Michael under the same bridge as before. They beat him up, broke several of his teeth, and caused blood to gush from his nose. Passersby discovered him and took him to nearby Jinnah Hospital, where a doctor gave him painkillers. After that attack, Michael decided to flee by himself to Goa, India, where his father's sister Josefin Saldanha lived. But he had only a forty-day visa to stay in India, so in January 2011 he was forced to return to Pakistan.

In April 2011, several of the mullahs and other men came to Michael's house and demanded that he come out. When Michael appeared, they began hitting him and said that they would "hang" him like Jesus. Two of the men stretched his arms out to the side, while others kicked him in the back. Michael was convinced they were going to kill him. A neighbor, Jaffer Khan, a Muslim, came out of his house and pleaded with the TTP members to let him live. Khan reminded the Muslims that Michael had small children, and he promised to educate Michael about Islam.

In July 2011, two TTP members arrived at Michael's house to investigate the status of his supposed Muslim "education" by Jaffer Khan. Michael refused to come out. One of the men, another mullah, said that if Michael were to go anywhere in Pakistan, they would be able to find him because of the strength and breadth of their network. In November 2011, Michael's uncle invited him to stay at his house in Lahore, Pakistan. Rosemary and their two children stayed in Karachi with her sister, Michelle Schroeder, who worked two kilometers from their house.

On January 6, 2012, Michelle did not come home at her usual time. Rosemary called Michelle's office. Her colleagues said that she had left the office on time. Rosemary then called both her parents and Michael to alert them. The next morning, someone threw a stone into the house with a paper wrapped around it that said Michelle had been kidnapped by a local mullah and that it would be better for them all if they were to accept Islam. The message further threatened that if they did not convert, the TTP would kill Michael and kidnap his wife and children. On January 7, 2012, Rosemary and Michelle's father, Kenneth Schroeder, went to the local police station to alert the authorities about Michelle's disappearance. The police told Schroeder that he should make the report in the district where she went missing, not his own district.

Five days later, on January 12, Michael returned from Lahore and went to the police station to report Michelle's kidnapping. The police refused to write a report once he told them that a TTP-affiliated mullah had kidnapped his sister-in-law. They even tore up the paper they were using to take notes and urged him to return to his home. They declared that they would not help and that there was no chance of forcing the mullahs to return Michelle.

Six days after the exchange at the police station, on January 18, Michael's sister-in-law, Magdalene D'Souza, wife of his brother Patrick, was abducted by TTP members. Magdalene, or Maggi, was with her two children on their way to a medical clinic near her house. When Maggi and the children did not return at her usual time that evening, her family began to search for them. A neighbor named Abbid told Michael that he had seen Maggi and the children being forced into a van. This was confirmed when a man associated with a local mullah visited Michael and told him that Mullahs Danish and Naqshbandi had kidnapped them. The man said, quite disquietingly, that Michael should not expect Maggi and the children to come back. Michael and Patrick went to the local Mahmudabad police station, but the police refused to file the complaint and pushed them out of the station.

The next month, February 2012, Maggi escaped from the mullahs' gang and ran to Michael's home. She reached Michael's door, but her TTP abductors forcibly dragged her away again. Michael was not at home, and Rosemary and the children were afraid to let her in. Two weeks later, Maggi escaped again and once more ran to Michael's house. Michael and Rosemary again did not let her in out of fear of the TTP. They spoke to her through the door. Maggi shouted: "Help me and save me! They are not good mullahs!" Rosemary recounted that her physical appearance was noticeably worrisome. She was wearing a niqab, a Muslim face covering that exposes only the eyes. Rosemary could see that Maggi's eyes were swollen with dark circles around them and one arm appeared to be broken. TTP members soon arrived, tearing her away as she continued to scream "Help me! Save me!"

After the traumatic experience of watching their sister-in-law abducted by Muslim extremists, Michael and Rosemary determined to move to a different neighborhood in Karachi called Karachi Cantonment. Unfortunately, it was not far enough away. In April 2012, Michael and Rosemary were spotted by a member of the same TTP gang. The very next day, TTP mullahs came to their house with a group of about twenty men. They demanded that Michael come out. After he did so, Rosemary closed the door behind him, took the children, and jumped from their house onto the roof of a neighboring house. The gang members, meanwhile, surrounded Michael and attacked him. During the assault, one of them declared: "Leave him, go for his family." A TTP member hit Michael on the back of the head with a gun, and Michael fell down unconscious. But the gang was unable to find Rosemary or their children, who had successfully escaped. The family later discovered Michael and took him to a hospital.

Once more, the D'Souzas decided to move, this time to the city of Larkana, almost three hundred miles from Karachi, where a friend of Michael's brother lived. This friend, Mickey, allowed Michael and his family to stay for six months. Yet neighbors started to get suspicious and began asking Mickey questions about this new family. Mickey recommended that Michael and his family leave Pakistan.

But that is an enormous step to take. So, in October 2012, Michael tried once more to find a safe place to live in his own country. He moved his family back to Karachi into yet another home, now in the working-class neighborhood of Gulshan-e-Iqbal. Rosemary's cousin Angela Clements, or Koki, had invited them to stay with her. The day after moving in, Michael went to St. Patrick Cathedral to visit a priest, Fr. Peter John. On his way to the cathedral, Michael passed the Madina Masjid Mosque in Gulshan-e-Iqbal. On the mosque wall were posters featuring a photograph of Michael. The posters read: "Michael committed blasphemy, insulted the Quran and the Prophet Muhammad. Michael deserves punishment. If you see this person contact ____." A phone number was listed. Michael ran back to Koki's house to tell his wife about the poster. Terrified, Michael and his family moved, in the middle of the night, to Hyderabad, a city about one hundred miles from Karachi, to stay with another family member, Irene Pinto. Irene and her son advised them, as others had, to leave Pakistan. Michael contacted Fr. Peter John and asked for his advice. The priest similarly urged him to flee Pakistan, arguing that the TTP's extensive network would continue to endanger Michael's family.

On November 21, 2012, Michael, Rosemary, their daughter Rochelle, and their son Miles flew to Bangkok with five hundred U.S. dollars in their pockets. There they hoped to apply for refugee status with the UNHCR. On December 14, Michael was given an asylum-seeker certificate, registered as "NI Number 15-12C00673." Four days later, Thai Immigration officials came to their Bangkok residence and arrested them. Though Michael and his family still had valid tourist visas, they were not staying at a hotel, a technical violation of the visa terms.[81] The family was taken to the Suan Phlu Immigration Detention Center, or IDC, where they were forced to pay fifty thousand Thai baht, or about fifteen hundred U.S. dollars, in order to be released. The D'Souzas acquired the money from a friend they had met at Holy Redeemer Redemptorist parish in central Bangkok shortly after their arrival in Thailand.

Almost a year later, on October 9, 2013, the D'Souzas had their interview with the UNHCR, called a Refugee Status Determination, or RSD. There were immediately problems with the RSD: the UNHCR required the family to use an interpreter because they were Pakistanis, even though Michael and his wife spoke English. Several times when Michael explained things in Urdu, the UNHCR-provided interpreter would translate Michael

---

[81] Thai police periodically round up asylum seekers across Bangkok, often as a means of soliciting "fines" from them or their often-Western sponsors in the city.

incorrectly. For example, Michael related that he had traveled to Lahore alone, but the interpreter told the UNHCR representative that Michael's entire family went with him. That was an important detail because Rosemary's sister had been kidnapped while she stayed with the D'Souzas. Worse, the interpreter told the UNHCR officer that Michael was lying. Multiple times, Michael tried to explain his side of the story in English, but the interpreter would interrupt him and order him to talk in Urdu, threatening to stop the interview and postpone it to another date. The UNHCR officer told Michael that he understood that he could speak English but that he should listen to the instructions of the interpreter. When the interview was over, the interpreter told Michael, in Urdu, that he should go back to Pakistan and become a Muslim, which would solve all his problems. The UN-HCR officer did not hear this.

After the disastrous UNHCR RSD, Michael and his family were forced to wait. Other Pakistani asylum seekers they met told them that it would likely be years before there was any outcome. And the chance that the UNHCR would rule in their favor and designate them refugees was not good. Moreover, their tourist visas had already expired.

The D'Souzas made the best of a bad situation. Almost immediately after their arrival in 2012, they developed friendships with several Catholics, some of them at Holy Redeemer, who were willing to provide them with financial and material support. One generous woman, a wealthy Filipina widow, paid to put them up in a small apartment for the equivalent of about sixty U.S. dollars per month. Rochelle and Miles were able to attend a local Thai school that had some English instruction. On August 2, 2014, Rosemary gave birth to a baby girl, Reine. At that point, they had already been in Thailand for almost two years.

My family arrived in Bangkok a few weeks before Reine was born.[82] Though I was encountering scores of Pakistani asylum seekers and refugees at Holy Redeemer, Michael, like Wilson, stood out. His very public practice of prayer after Mass made an impression. His presence at the church was also constant, unlike that of many others who visited the church only during weekend Masses, when they could implore parishioners for financial contributions. Michael's teenage daughter was an altar server, which suggested a deeper family commitment to Christ and His Church.

One day in the fall of 2014, I introduced myself to Michael, his wife, and their three children. Michael acknowledged that he, like so many others, had fled persecution at the hands of Muslim extremists. He related that he and his family were barely scraping by, adding that the money needed to pay for his older daughter's education alone was the equivalent of 120 U.S. dollars a month. I didn't offer money. We had just met, and I was afraid that one donation might open the floodgate to petitions from similar Pakistanis if word got around.

Then I did not see Michael or his family again for several weeks. I discovered from another Pakistani Catholic that they had been arrested by the Thai police again and taken to the IDC. I did not know that this was not their first time in that infamous and overcrowded place. Within a few weeks, friends from the parish again paid the fee necessary to release the D'Souzas, and I started seeing Michael at Mass again. I approached him

[82] Many of the details in this section can be found in Casey Chalk, "A Witness in Bangkok: An Anniversary in Exile," *New Oxford Review* 83, no. 10 (December 2016).

and told him I knew about what had happened to him and his family. I mentioned that I had written a few articles for American publications, some Catholic, and would be willing to try to get his story published for American audiences. Michael eagerly agreed.

A weekday evening not long after, I took the long trip from the center of the city to Michael's apartment. It was the wet season and raining heavily, so I took the underground train, the MRT, several stops, jumped in a cab in bumper-to-bumper rush-hour traffic, hopped on a motorbike taxi to an agreed-upon meeting place, and then took yet more motorbike taxis with Michael to his apartment building. The trip took an hour and a half. This was a commute Michael made almost daily, on a bicycle no less, in order to visit our Redemptorist parish.

When Michael and I entered the elevator, I noticed an icon of Jesus prominently taped inside atop its doors. This was curious in a part of town populated primarily by working-class, predominantly Buddhist Thais. I asked Michael about it, and he readily acknowledged that he had placed it there. On the eighth floor, where Michael lived, every wall and threshold was likewise covered in Catholic iconography arranged by Michael, perhaps as a bulwark against spiritual attack.

The apartment itself was very humble. The cement floor was covered by a few area rugs. There was a small kitchen, one bedroom, and a small common living area, where they had placed additional small beds for family members. They had a small patio overlooking the city. Michael and I sat outside and talked and drank tea while Rosemary prepared traditional Pakistani fare, spicy biryani, nihari, and naan. We ate, sitting on the floor, while Michael and Rosemary related an almost unbelievable story of being arrested and detained in the IDC.

A squad of Thai policemen had arrived at their apartment building, acting on orders to round up illegal asylum seekers. Michael, his family standing behind him and filled with trepidation, opened the door to greet the man commissioned to take them away. The officer paused before passing the threshold. "I feel as if something has touched me," he stammered. Michael and his family stood and waited, also confused. The policeman considered stepping forward, hesitated once more, and relented. "I am here to take you away, but I do not want to enter your home," he admitted. He retreated to the elevator and to his commanding officer.

The commanding officer returned with his subordinate. His determined resolution also quickly turned to anxiety and uncertainty. "I do not want to enter into this home; there is something here," the officer explained confusedly to Michael, who was himself just as bewildered. "We have a quota to meet — show us where others like you are staying, and we will take them instead of your family." Michael refused. "How can I give up another family of Christians?" he asked rhetorically. "You must take us. Our time has come. It is finished."

The reluctant police officers escorted Michael and his family to the IDC. While the family awaited their fate — to be consigned indefinitely to a jail cell until their fine was paid — the commanding officer made sure they were placed in a waiting room with air conditioning, a notable luxury in Thailand. The officer then returned with a variety of prepared foods. "We do not need this food," confessed Michael. "Please give it to the hungry prisoners who have been here much longer than us." The police officer became angry. "I have bought this food for you from my own money! I know there is something special about you, and I want whatever power it is that you have. You must accept this gift."[83] Michael again refused. "I will not take any special treatment." The officer became verbally and physically abusive, and he quickly threw Michael, his wife, and their three children into crowded cells full of illegal immigrants. Michael and his son, Miles, were separated from Rosemary and the two daughters, per IDC regulations.

In order to feed their nine-month-old daughter, Rosemary shared tins of baby formula with several other mothers. Michael, in turn, took to what he does best: praying. In an act of courage—given that the jail cell was filled with Catholics, Evangelicals, and Muslims—Michael knelt and prayed aloud the Rosary and the Divine Mercy Chaplet. Fellow prisoners were at first curious, then derogatory. One Evangelical inmate told Michael that he was praying to idols. Michael responded: "Don't you keep pictures of your deceased family members, both to remember them and honor them? I keep these images because they are my family." On another occasion, he explained to questioning inmates that his Rosary prayers could all be found in the pages of the New Testament.

Michael would also accompany the Evangelicals in their own prayers. Soon prisoners of all faiths—even Muslims—were joining Michael in his prayers, at first kneeling and listening, and

---

[83] Such a statement from a Thai policeman likely will seem strange to Westerners, but Thais are a peculiarly superstitious people very attuned to the spirit world. For example, Thais often prefer cesarean sections over natural deliveries so that they can consult a soothsayer beforehand in order to have their child born on an "auspicious" day. There are also shrines throughout the country built to honor the spirits that inhabit specific locations, and Thais make offerings of incense sticks, food, and drink (including bottles of Fanta) to appease those spirits.

eventually reciting the Rosary alongside him. A Bangladeshi Muslim named Abdul requested that Michael intercede for him, as he deeply missed his family. Michael agreed. A week later, Abdul was informed that a flight had been arranged for him to return to his native country. Then Michael's teenage daughter had a dream in which Jesus appeared to her and urged her to get ready because her time had come to depart the IDC. A few days later, a parishioner arrived at the IDC and handed over the full fee — fourteen hundred U.S. dollars — required to free the entire family.[84]

Michael's courage to pray in the IDC stemmed from his experience as a religious minority in Pakistan, which he also related to me during that evening we spent together in his apartment. Michael escorted me, with my writing pad full of notes, down the elevator and out onto the street. On the long, silent taxi drive home, I thought, prayed, and wept.

Over the next several months, I wrote about Michael. His story was published in *New Oxford Review* in December 2016. But my family's relationship with Michael and his family continued to grow. Once, after Sunday Mass, Michael approached my family selling rosaries. One of my wife's friends, who had professional experience with the Pakistani asylum-seeking community, was suspicious. I told her that he was my friend and that I trusted him. I think the rosaries were about three U.S. dollars each. In retrospect, knowing everything I do now about Michael and his suffering, I regret that I did not buy them all. Indeed, Michael and his family's story might seem unbelievable, but the longer one knows another man, and the more one learns how he can

---

[84] The bail fee at the IDC varied in U.S. currency because of the fluctuating exchange rate.

be trusted, the harder it becomes to reject that man's claims, no matter how fantastic they might be. I do not doubt anything Michael told me, particularly because of what happened to him and his family over the next year and a half.

On March 9, 2015, Thai immigration police once more arrested the D'Souza family and placed them in the IDC. And once again, friends paid to have them bailed out, and on March 27, they were released. In July, the UNHCR notified them that their refugee application had been rejected because the D'Souza's explanation of the attacks by the TTP gang was not sufficiently clear. Nor, the UNHCR explained, were the details about the kidnapping of Michelle and Maggi clear or consistent. The UN-HCR added that they did not believe Michael's story about the poster at the Karachi mosque labeling him a blasphemer. His family submitted an appeal to the UNHCR in October, which was rejected a year later, on September 30, 2016.

Through all these trials, Michael and his family remained resolutely faithful. Though they complained plenty about their mistreatment at the hands of Pakistani extremists and about a UNHCR bureaucratic process that seemed prejudiced against them, they never complained about the many other indignities they faced daily. Perhaps the greatest of these was that Michael and Rosemary were so dependent on others for charity. The little money they earned came from generous parishioners at Holy Redeemer who paid them to clean their homes. Several times, when I gave a few dollars to other Pakistani asylum seekers, they would complain and frown, uttering "too little, too little." Not Michael and his family. They accepted anything they were given without complaint. For them, Michael told me, it was all a gift from God.

The humiliations endured by Michael and his family served, and still serve for me, as a testament to a family caught up in a story of redemption far greater than themselves. His wife readily admitted that she had often been a reluctant participant in prayer, and her experience in Pakistan and Thailand had drawn her, if slowly and with much hesitation, closer to Christ. Her faith was further tested once their appeal to the UNHCR was rejected. At that point, Michael and his family no longer had any legal standing in Thailand. Their options were few, and all were bad. They could return to Pakistan, where they would undoubtedly encounter renewed persecution and possibly even death. They could try to hide from Thai immigration authorities, perhaps with some family from Holy Redeemer, though this would put such a family at legal peril. (I was not willing to accept such a risk to my Thai visa.) Or Michael and his family could turn themselves in and endure indefinite confinement in the IDC.

Michael decided their chances of survival were better in the IDC than in Pakistan. Someone had advised him, wrongly, that the UNHCR would reopen the D'Souza's case if they returned to the detention center. And so, in October 2016, Michael reported to the IDC with his family in tow, humbly accepting their uncertain fate. The last text message I received from him before the Thai authorities confiscated his cell phone read as follows: "All are going inside IDC, my wife and 3 children also with me. Please pray for us. Amen."

Michael had become, like St. Paul, a "prisoner for Christ Jesus," an "ambassador in chains" (Eph. 3:1, 6:20).

4

The Immigration Detention Center

For it is for thy sake that I have borne reproach,
that shame has covered my face.
I have become a stranger to my brethren,
an alien to my mother's sons.
For zeal for thy house has consumed me,
and the insults of those who insult thee
have fallen on me.

—Psalm 69:7–9

Bangkok's Suan Phlu Immigration Detention Center, or IDC, has achieved international notoriety for its corruption and inhumanity. According to a 2012 report by Human Rights Watch, or HRW,[85] detainees described the jail's "lack of ventilation, lack of recreation, mixing of children and adults, poor food, and abusive treatment by guards." A thirty-year-old Burmese man reported being punched while getting fingerprinted because "I couldn't

---

[85] Human Rights Watch, *Ad Hoc and Inadequate: Thailand's Treatment of Refugees and Asylum Seekers* (New York: Human Rights Watch, 2012), https://www.hrw.org/report/2012/09/12/ad-hoc-and-inadequate/thailands-treatment-refugees-and-asylum-seekers.

stop my fingers from moving." A lawyer who represents many detainees described life at the IDC: "They are only allowed out of their cells twice a week. The medical facilities are limited and counselors from the Bangkok Refugee Center are only allowed in twice a month to provide psycho-social counseling."

The lawyer noted that conditions for female detainees were particularly inhumane. One mother who was pregnant with her second child at the time of her detention remembered her experience:

> I was eight months pregnant. I had spent one-and-a-half months in the IDC. I couldn't eat the Thai food. I was really suffering. I slept on the floor with no blanket. It was the room for women and children. There were 200 people in that room. There was no space. I couldn't sleep for four or five days. There were only two toilets for 200 people. It was not clean. We were only allowed two hours in the courtyard every three days.
>
> One of the detainees beat my daughter. He was crazy. There was no guard, no police to help us. She was not injured. UNHCR didn't help. They said, "We are not involved in the IDC." I paid myself to get out of the IDC. I paid all the money I had for bail.

Another woman, thirty-three years old, claimed that the male Thai guards at the IDC often had sex with female detainees, and that the sanitary conditions were intolerable:

> That room was only for 20 people, but we had 80 to 100 in there. We slept foot to head with the others. During that time in the IDC, we didn't have a toilet door. It was just open. If you take showers, people can see your whole

body.... Also, in the jail it was just for women, but the guards were all men. They'd come at improper times. The policemen would come at night. They would come to the IDC and hug closely the women who were dressed in barely any clothes. The police were also close with some of the prisoner women there. They'd come to talk with the other prisoner women and make relationships with them, like husband and wife.... If you put water in [to the toilet] everything would just overflow and come out again. I couldn't go to the toilet because the smell was so bad. So I didn't eat anything because if I ate then I'd have to go to the toilet. It was an evil place.

This is the place Michael D'Souza was forced to take his children to in October 2016 when their application for refugee status was denied.[86]

My wife, Claire, first started going to the IDC prior to the D'Souza's arrival there in 2016. She would go with a Mormon friend whose church had formed a group that went every week. The group, largely composed of middle-aged women, named themselves ESTiN (Expats Supporting Those in Need) and held annual fundraisers to raise money to bail out detainees.

The entrance of the IDC was reminiscent of a United Nations conference. Every weekday, Thais, Pakistanis, Africans (mostly Somalis and Nigerians), Central Asians, and an assortment of Westerners would arrive at 10:00 a.m. to visit people they knew and bring them food or other necessities. Visitors had a very short window of time to register, so they often arrived more than an

---

[86] Many of the details in this section can be found in Casey Chalk, "Letter to the Editor: Update on Pakistani Catholics," *New Oxford Review* 84, no. 1 (January–February 2017).

hour before the IDC opened to stand in line, sometimes with a hundred people, to submit the necessary paperwork to request access. If anything on the form was bureaucratically amiss, the IDC official would demand that the applicant go to the back of the line, which might mean he would not make it in.

In February 2016, the BBC published a controversial video by one of their investigative teams, secretly filmed inside the IDC.[87] The BBC team decided to film covertly inside the IDC because Thai authorities prohibit visitors, including journalists and human-rights organizations, from touring the entire facility.[88] But after the 2016 BBC IDC exposé, security was tightened. Visitors had to submit their names and passport numbers days in advance of their visit; and their group had to be sponsored by a church or another organization. (More seasoned regulars suggested that visitors change their phone number and address slightly to avoid calls from detainees or even possibly IDC officials. Sure enough, after Claire's first visit, she began getting nightly calls from a random detainee she had visited.)

After registering, visitors had to wait an hour before they were allowed in. Claire and the other women would go across the street to a café, where they assembled bags of food (especially fresh fruit, a rare pleasure) and personal-hygiene products. Often the group would commission a fellow church member of Pakistani origin to cook homemade comfort food early that morning.

[87] "Secret Filming in Thai Detention Centre," BBC News, February 26, 2016, https://www.bbc.com/news/av/magazine-35654117/secret-filming-in-thai-detention-centre.

[88] Many of those involved in human rights work in Thailand resented the BBC video as it elicited a strong, negative response from Thai authorities, which made the work of those helping detained asylum-seekers even more difficult.

Once the authorities finally allowed visitors in, they would bark at them to move from place to place and often capriciously reject various items that people had brought. No SIM cards were allowed, nor anything that could be used to cut hair, which I didn't understand.

Once inside, the scene was hectic, overwhelming, terribly hot, and full of mosquitos. There was an open drain that ran on the edge of the visiting room that smelled foul. Scores of prisoners in blaze-orange, IDC-issued T-shirts would be corralled into a long hall behind a seven-foot-high wire fence to see their visitors. Visitors were separated from detainees by another seven-foot-high fence, with a short, one-yard space in between for guards to stroll and pass money or paperwork between sides. Officials let in as many as sixty visitors at a time, which made conversations difficult to hear as people shouted back and forth their various requests and updates.

My wife and I began visiting Michael and his family soon after they entered the IDC. Michael, his wife, and his thirteen-year-old daughter would update us on news regarding their internment, including his daughter's eye infection, their poor sleeping conditions, and the graft that defined their daily existence. Michael, now sporting a bushy "haji" beard, told us that guards did not allow razors in the IDC but charged the equivalent of fifteen U.S. dollars to shave any willing men. Outside the IDC a haircut in Bangkok usually cost the equivalent of two or three U.S. dollars. Now I understood the restriction on hair-cutting items.

Michael's wife tried to share some of the details of their many struggles but broke down. Michael's most generous sponsor in Bangkok, a Filipina woman and devout Catholic, was there as well, and she exhorted them to trust in Christ, unite their sufferings to the Cross, and to entrust all their needs to "Mama Maria." She led them in prayer and several hymns, their voices momentarily raised above the shouting in the hall. The smile of Michael's daughter, Rochelle, was radiant during this entire exchange, her innocent hazel eyes serving as their own testament to an unwavering faith and courage that no hardship seemed capable of dispelling.

As I tried my best to maintain my composure, I noticed a back room with glass walls directly beyond the detainees. A Thai police officer, seated at his computer with his back to me, was playing the then-popular game Candy Crush. Could the discrepancy between these two realities, separated by only a few yards, have been more stark?

The D'Souzas' Filipina sponsor cheered through the metal wiring, "Think how many souls you are saving with your suffering!" She was rewarded with simple, unflappable assent. These Pakistanis were tough stuff.

The whole meeting lasted only about twenty minutes. We waved our goodbyes to the D'Souzas and made our way back outside to the busy Suan Phlu Street. We were free, free to go wherever we liked, free to *live*. Michael and his family were not.

☞

The experience of visiting the IDC was emotionally draining but spiritually potent and always catechetical.[89] For example, the ecumenical response to Bangkok's asylum-seeker crisis was

---

[89] Many of the details in this section can be found in Casey Chalk, "Jesus in Thailand: The Christian Asylum Seekers of Bangkok," *Touchstone* (May/June 2018), https://www.touchstonemag.com/archives/article.php?id=31-03-018-c.

inspiring. The ESTiN group maintained an extensive log of all the detainees they knew inside and of when those detainees had last been visited. Although many were Mormon, many others were Catholic, Evangelical, Orthodox, and even Muslim.

Once, while exchanging high-decibel words with our Pakistani friends through the wire fence, I noticed a group of young American Evangelicals reading Scripture to a group of Pakistani Evangelical asylum seekers — in Urdu, with an Urdu-language Bible. A woman from our Catholic parish periodically led a group of French Charismatic Catholics to visit inmates.

Another time, in the small café across the street, I met an Evangelical missionary from Texas who had brought along his teenage children. "I want them to see this, so they understand how much an American passport is really worth," he told me.

Over time, we also began exposing other friends and relatives to the IDC. Jon and Crissy, a couple who lived in our building and attended Holy Redeemer, had three teenagers, two of whom were altar servers. At one point over dinner, we shared the D'Souzas' story with them. Jon was enthusiastic about coming with us to the IDC, and after witnessing the intimidation by Thai IDC officials, the sight of scores of desperate asylum seekers, and the conversation and prayers with the D'Souzas, he asked how they could help. "Keep coming," we said.

Soon thereafter, we brought Jon, Crissy, and their two older boys to the IDC (they judged that the experience would be too traumatic for their young daughter). As we stood in line to see the D'Souzas, I suddenly realized that his sons might recognize Michael's daughter Rochelle, as she also had been an altar server at Holy Redeemer. What a bizarre experience for a middle-class American teenager, to do extracurricular church activities with a female acquaintance and then visit her in a detention center.

The Persecuted

The boys were overwhelmed, confused, almost speechless. The younger son, who immediately recognized Rochelle, tried to start a conversation with her but quickly realized he did not know what to ask or say to a peer who spent every day locked up. He couldn't really ask a fellow teenager what she did for fun — in jail. Rochelle, however, was beaming, as she always seemed to be, and tried to keep the conversation going, graciously asking *him* how he was doing, what he was up to, how he was enjoying school, if he was still an altar server.

My wife's parents, Stephen and Christine, had met both Michael's and Wilson's families during their first two visits to Thailand in 2015. Early in 2016, they had begun contributing money for Rochelle's schooling. They had also read with great interest the growing number of articles I had written about the asylum-seeker crisis in Bangkok and were eager to see Michael and his family when they returned to Thailand in February 2017.

That month, they twice visited the IDC with us. The first time Steve and Christine came with us, the guards inexplicably pulled out all kinds of items as contraband: holy water, religious items, and strawberry milk for Michael's baby daughter, among them. Christine also observed that the cooked Pakistani food that was brought to detainees had been sitting out since the morning and likely would not be eaten until well after we had left the IDC. Someone would have to be desperate to eat that, she thought. Had anyone gotten food poisoning from eating it?

Steve had seen the BBC video of the inside of the IDC and thought he was prepared to see things firsthand. But he had not anticipated the heavy atmosphere of depression and helplessness, he later remarked. Both visitors and the visited seemed demoralized. "These people were visiting the IDC without bringing any hope with them," observed Steve, who said it reminded him of the inscription above the entrance to Hell described in Dante's *Divine Comedy*: "All hope abandon, ye who enter here."

Pressed up against the metal chain-link fence in order to find the D'Souzas on the other side, both Steve and Christine were frustrated as they shouted over the cacophony and din caused by everyone else's yelling. "About the best I could do was to tell Michael that we were praying for him," noted Christine. When they stepped back from the front row of visitors, they were unable to hear what the D'Souzas said. Both were amazed that visitors were willing to hand over rolled-up cash to IDC guards, who would then hand the money over to detainees. It seemed an obvious way to encourage graft in the system, with guards collecting a "commission."

Steve and Christine were dismayed by the conditions at the IDC: "Horrible, hot, dirty, crowded," said Christine. "They all had bug bites and rashes. Michael had no shoes and we brought flip flops for him.... We heard from the D'Souzas and other visitors that the drinking water was often dirty and made people sick." Christine could also tell that the baby, Reine, was suffering in the heat and damp conditions with a visible rash on her skin.

After trying to talk with the D'Souzas, we all prayed a Rosary with them. "There was overwhelming sadness for the state that they were in and the fact that we could do so little," Christine remarked later. Steve, overwhelmed by the whole experience, retreated to sit on a bench, weighed down by the gloom and inhumanity in front of him. Christine's thoughts on her first visit to the IDC are worth quoting in full:

> The sad fact that we could do nothing significant for them was overwhelming. Rosemary was clearly grateful that we had come to see them, but her prayers were accompanied by tears. They had been in long enough that they all were

suffering from the heat, the dirt, the lack of any certainty that this would achieve anything but misery. My sense was that all of this was not fair and did not make a bit of difference. This was happening in 2017. Not back in the history books, but today. My heart broke for them, but they were stuck in a horrible system at the mercy of a seemingly unfeeling government.

Indeed, for a couple of months during the D'Souzas' stay, the Thai government refused to allow anyone to post bail unless they were going to be immediately deported to their home country.

There were other, far-reaching frustrations with the Thai government. The Mormon women's group ESTiN had planned to hold a large fundraiser at a major hotel in Bangkok. Unfortunately, in the wake of Thai king Bhumipol Aduladej's death in October 2016, the event had to be canceled. No celebrations or events could be held during the national mourning time, during which many Thais wore black every day. That mourning period lasted an entire year. Could the many beneficiaries of ESTiN's charity, including the D'Souza's, go an entire year without that additional money?

There were a few small bright spots. Michael and Rosemary mentioned one specific IDC guard who was responsive to them, who was "good and kind" to them. The D'Souzas were also able to persuade the Thai officials to grant their son, Miles, permission to stay with the Filipina woman who frequently visited them in the IDC. Miles had some health problems, and the poor conditions inside the IDC provided enough justification to get him out in late February 2017. It meant Miles could attend school and have a less traumatic daily life.

The rest of the family, unfortunately, had no idea when their ordeal would be over.

5

Heroes and Villains

Therefore you have no excuse, O man,
whoever you are, when you judge another;
for in passing judgment upon him
you condemn yourself, because you,
the judge, are doing the very same things.

—Romans 2:1

There are many Pakistani asylum seekers and refugees in Thailand, probably somewhere between seven thousand and twelve thousand people. Most of them are Catholics and Evangelical Christians. They are particularly visible on Saturday evenings and Sundays, when they descend on Bangkok's churches, looking for sympathetic souls willing to offer charity for their many needs: food, clothing, medicine, and so forth. All are impoverished. Some are more aggressive than others in their begging, especially if an unknowing American ex-pat establishes the precedent of handing money directly over to them, rather than going through the various church ministries that have been established to provide basic necessities to this community.

Holy Redeemer, my family's Redemptorist parish in Bangkok, had a complex relationship with its large asylum-seeker community.[90] Located in the central part of the city, Holy Redeemer had become a haven for refugees and asylum seekers mostly from Pakistan, but with contingents from elsewhere in Asia and Africa. For years, a lay parish movement, which enjoyed explicit support from a few of the parish priests, had provided all manner of foodstuffs to more than four hundred such families, collecting donations from willing parishioners on most Sundays. Moreover, the food bank put several Pakistanis to work, collecting the money and arranging distribution of the materials to needy families. This charity, though praiseworthy, was unfortunately not enough for many of these poor wayfarers. Many required medical treatment, especially the elderly and mothers with young children. Living conditions for many of these people were terrible.

Often on Sundays, the needy anxiously awaited the end of Mass as an opportunity to impress their requests upon potential benefactors. Their persistence, their lack of tact, and their sometimes aggressive tactics were often jarring, particularly to those unfamiliar with the parish. Indeed, typically the destitute had success only with sympathetic Western visitors. Many parishioners did not like these people and preferred that they be excluded from the church's life and practice.

Some of this disfavor likely stemmed from a justified resentment: many Thais, and many Thai Catholics, live in poverty, particularly in the country's more remote provinces. And with the recent significant demographic shift in Bangkok's Catholic population, Thai Catholics probably felt a certain pique toward

---

[90] Many of the details in this section can be found in Casey Chalk, "The Day My Pastor Defended the Poor and the Stranger," *Ethika Politika*, August 9, 2017, https://ethikapolitika.org/2017/08/09/day-pastor-defended-poor-stranger.

South Asians and Africans who, to a degree, distracted the Church from the needs of the country's own poor. This resentment felt by many Thai Catholics at Holy Redeemer appeared even to have reached the level of the parish's Thai clergy. In spring 2017, I observed a new sign prominently displayed in the vestibule alongside Mass times and other parish news. It read:

> Announcement for Safety and Security Issue: Due to many incident reports from our parishioners that there are groups of people who come to our church ground and request for financial assistance from our parishioners, many felt threatened and disturbed when they were approached by these people in the toilets, parking lot, underground parking as well as in the church while they are praying and during religious services. We are aware of this issue and are handling it in due process. In the meantime, please watch out for your own safety and security.

While a certain measure of frustration was understandable — I myself had been approached while in the restroom — describing members of the parish community as "groups of people" seemed to unnecessarily and uncharitably abstract them. Were they not our brothers and sisters in Christ? It also seemed hyperbolic that parishioners were complaining of feeling "threatened" by people asking for money when almost all such petitioners were abject-looking mothers, often with their young children in tow.

More to the point, where, besides in church or outside in the parking lot, could poverty-stricken Catholics be expected to have an opportunity to ask for help? I began to wonder whether my church leaders were more concerned about the opinions of influential individuals and families at the parish or with heeding Christ's call to care for the poor, the sick, and the widowed.

The Persecuted

Had they forgotten the words of St. Ambrose, who so famously exhorted the Church: "If you have two shirts in your closet, one belongs to you and the other to the man with no shirt"?

But one humid Sunday, the pastor of our parish ascended the ambo and began to talk about "people coming to the parish asking for money." His words were potent, straightforward, and decidedly forceful:

> Many people have complained to me, sending me e-mails, writing texts, calling on the phone, visiting my office, about the people begging for money. I understand that it can be frustrating or uncomfortable. But in this time of war and suffering, this is the lot of every big city in the world. There are refugees and asylum seekers everywhere in need of help. Jesus told us that the poor would always be with us, and that is how I see this crisis. But you should remember that these people come not only for money, but they also come to pray, to receive the Eucharist, for fellowship. I will not refuse these to them. If you want, please help them. If not, you will have to suffer through and endure it. The poor will always be with us, and they are not going away.

When so many Christians are suffering persecution and deprivation around the world, this was the message we needed to hear. The poor and the stranger place upon all of us petitions that are often inconvenient, frustrating, or even rude. But as Jesus told us, they are manifestations of His Mystical Body: "'Lord, when did we see thee hungry or thirsty or a stranger or naked or sick or in prison, and did not minister to thee?' Then he will answer them, 'Truly, I say to you, as you did it not to one of the least of these, you did it not to me'" (Matt. 25:44–45). We will be judged for how well we sought to care for them.

⌒

The deeper Claire and I immersed ourselves in the Bangkok asylum-seeker crisis, the more we realized how ignorant we were about all its frustrating complexities. Wilson recommended that we meet with Fr. John Murray, an Augustinian priest who worked for Caritas, the body responsible for the social action of the Thai Catholic Church under the Catholic Bishops' Conference of Thailand (CBCT). Caritas was on the front lines of the Thai Catholic Bishops' Conference response to the asylum-seeker crisis.

I invited Fr. John to dinner at our apartment, telling him that I was eager to discuss the Pakistani asylum-seeker crisis in Bangkok. He graciously accepted.

Fr. John is a big, tall Australian from Brisbane with a quirky sense of humor and eccentric spiritual interests (one of his favorite spiritual writers is French Jesuit Pierre Teilhard de Chardin, some of whose writings were condemned by the Holy Office for doctrinal errors). But we soon came to appreciate the degree to which Fr. John understood the asylum-seeker crisis. He had been working for Caritas Thailand since 2006, providing pastoral care of the refugee population and volunteers, helping to network for urban asylum-seekers and refugees, and working to increase the level of outreach to that community. He worked closely with other NGOs, faith-based communities, international schools, and individuals through a grassroots network group called Bangkok Asylum Seeker and Refugee Assistance Network (BASRAN), which reaches out to the vulnerable population and seeks to understand how best to serve their educational, medical, and financial needs, including employment. The main players, apart from the UNHCR and Caritas Thailand, were Jesuit Refugee

Service, Asylum Access Thailand (which provided legal services), and Tzu Chi (a Taiwanese Buddhist foundation offering medical outreach), among others. Fr. John would make pastoral visits to a Bangkok prison for Mass, as well as offer counseling and arrange material assistance for the needy.

Given that experience, Fr. John was uniquely suited to explain the complexities of the asylum-seeker crisis to us.[91] What he described was bureaucratically frustrating. Fr. John had been working in the crisis so long and understood so deeply the many difficulties faced by all parties that he was not eager to criticize any particular person or group for failing to do their part. I viewed the UNHCR as failing persecuted Pakistani Catholics. Fr. John viewed them as do-gooders who were helplessly understaffed and underfunded. He did not agree that the UNHCR was biased against Pakistani Christians. He explained that the present political realities of the world were making the work of the UNHCR much more difficult and restricting its impact to a significant degree. He noted that, in Bangkok, the UNHCR spoke no longer about resettlement of refugees but, rather, community development, because everyone had to acknowledge that these thousands of asylum seekers would be in Thailand for a long time, despite the fact that the government does not recognize "illegal aliens" and that they are therefore unable to find legal employment.

Moreover, Fr. John dealt with a much broader constituency than just Pakistanis, who made up only 50 percent of the total

---

[91] Many of the details in this section can be found in Fr. John Murray, O.S.A., "Letter to the Editor: The West's Refusal to Acknowledge Brutalities," *New Oxford Review* 85, no. 6 (July–August 2018).

asylum-seeker population. Pakistanis, said Fr. John, were the most readily identified as they often were the most vocal in expressing themselves and their needs. They also had strong international backing. But asylum seekers also hailed from Sri Lanka, Syria, Congo, Somalia, Iraq, Vietnam, Cambodia, Laos, China, and Palestine, among other places. They came because of war, persecution, and other domestic travails, noted Fr. John. He also explained the psychological trauma stemming from what they experienced in their native countries and from the culture shock associated with fleeing to a new culture, especially one that technically did not want them. Thai policy toward asylum seekers, explained Fr. John, was not bound by the U.N. Convention on Refugees, so the Thai government did not recognize asylum seekers and refugees as such and could define them however they pleased.

Fr. John argued that the asylum seekers in Bangkok did not constitute a "large population," particularly in a major city of more than 10 million people. But it seemed large because they were such a desperate population with such a high level of need. "Their level of need is overwhelming," he agreed.

There were no easy answers to the crisis, Fr. John explained. Nevertheless, we were grateful for the conversation and eager to continue it. Fr. John agreed to let me visit his office in a quieter part of Bangkok; so, several weeks later, I found myself in a Caritas compound that provided meals, English-language education, and counseling services to perhaps hundreds of asylum seekers and refugees every day.

After ten years of working for Caritas, Fr. John had developed a mature, tempered suspicion toward the many asylum seekers who came to him for help. The great majority, he readily admitted, had indeed experienced tremendous suffering. He did not doubt that many had been the objects of persecution. But he had also come to understand that many people had come less because they were genuinely concerned for their lives and more because Bangkok, with its lax immigration laws and large expat community, was simply a place with more financial opportunities. Many Pakistanis in Bangkok were best identified as economic migrants seeking a better opportunity. "A good aim in life," remarked Fr. John. "Their mistake is that they made an unwise choice in seeking their life goal as they are not refugees under UNHCR guidelines."

Nevertheless, even this "unwise choice," sometimes done on the basis of receiving bad advice or "being tempted to do so by fellow countrymen with an agenda," brought some benefits. A South Asian living in abject poverty was a nobody in his or her home country. If that person immigrated to Bangkok, he or she could at least claim status as the victim of mistreatment. That did not mean an end to poverty, but it did mean occasional free food, sympathy from hoodwinked expats, and perhaps even a shot at a new life as a bona fide refugee placed in a third country.

Unfortunately, this also led to what Fr. John called the "dependency trap." Once a person gets used to relying on others for his livelihood, it can be normalized. Fr. John had met such people in his many years working in Bangkok.

Fr. John pondered the question: "Is it that they cannot return home, or they will not?" He had a significant number of Pakistanis who had their case for refugee status rejected who would still not hear anything about returning home. Rather, they chose to stay in Bangkok without status under the UNHCR or the government, a difficult life of interminable limbo that, over time, causes new dilemmas. What would they do if they wanted to get married? How would they register their children born in Thailand? "Is

life that bad back home?... I do not understand it," remarked
Fr. John with incredulity.

Moreover, he explained, people in the church whom Fr. John
knew and trusted had told him that life back home was certainly
bad but not *entirely* desperate. The reason such persons refused to
return even after their case was rejected, reasoned Fr. John, was
"loss of face." Indeed, many came on behalf of their families to
seek resettlement through the refugee path. "This was not just for
them but to act as a gate for others in their family to follow. So,
they have failed their family." Few wanted to return to Pakistan
empty-handed failures.

Indeed, while I was visiting Fr. John that day, I recognized
someone from Holy Redeemer walking the grounds of the facility. I could tell by Fr. John's body language and careful choice of
words that he was not fond of this person and did not trust her.
Being the good priest, he refused to go into much detail. But he
did explain how the reasons she gave for coming to Thailand
had changed over the years — religious persecution, suffering as
a political dissident, a dangerous personal situation. Was all that
true? Perhaps. Or maybe she had discovered a way to manipulate
people into helping her live a better life in Bangkok.

But as Fr. John also observed, "the reality is that some do find
work or find ways to gainfully use their time, one way or another.
They do earn a livelihood and find a purpose while here." Such
persons became "a sign of hope for the others who linger, looking
to others for long-term help." Indeed, some even earned a level of
success in their work or in helping others in their niche asylum-
seeker community. Such migrants, he explained, were people
who "have enough energy and commitment to leave their home
to make more of their life or to be able to say enough is enough.
These people show initiative and would be great contributors

to any society." After lunch at a nearby Thai restaurant, I said goodbye to Fr. John and made the long journey back toward the city center.[92]

Over three years working in Bangkok, I encountered my fair share of heroes and villains caught up in the asylum-seeker crisis, from corrupt Thai police officials to my parish pastor and Fr. John Murray. Yet sometimes the line between heroes and villains was blurry. And sometimes, when dealing with the desperate and needy, it required effort and shrewdness to determine how desperate and needy such people truly were.

Given my family's limited available time and resources to help our parish's poor and persecuted, those seemed determinations worth making. I know I myself can be that same desperate and needy person, trying to represent myself in the best possible light, when I know deep down how sinful, how wretched, how

[92] Fr. John shared with me the following entry from his personal journal, written in March 2008, only two years after he began working for Caritas. As he told me, it provides the initial context for his now decade-and-a-half-long pastoral journey.

In urban refugees in Bangkok, I have found something that energizes me, that inspires me, that makes me want to take some risks. Who are these people? I now present three cases I am helping: A Somali male, an Iraqi male, and a Cambodian woman. These are just examples of people that are just so desperate. They leave one hostile, fearful environment to find themselves in another. They are here where they are not wanted and where they have no standing. They have no money and no work and really no home. Where can they turn for help? A few NGOs, but so little help is available for them and they need so much. My heart goes out to them. I find that as I share their story, other people are touched too and want to help.

manipulative I can be. Nevertheless, though I can be stingy, Jesus, with His love and grace, is not. Christ, who sees me for who I truly am, in all the complexity of my heroism and villainy, never refuses to welcome me home. Perhaps there are worse errors than being too gracious with the impoverished people we encounter.

6

Rescuing the D'Souzas from the IDC

*And when he had spoken thus, he knelt down and prayed with
them all. And they all wept and embraced Paul and kissed him,
sorrowing most of all because of the word he had spoken, that they
should see his face no more. And they brought him to the ship.*

— Acts 20:36–38

"We cannot stay here any longer! We want to go back to Pakistan!"[93] Michael D'Souza shouted his decision to me through
the wire fence above the din at the IDC. I was surprised by this
sudden determination. Michael and his family had entered the
IDC on October 17, 2016, and had survived eight months there,
convinced that the facility was better than the dangers they faced
in Pakistan. They prayed that God would work some miracle, a
reward for their faith and perseverance in the face of persecution
at home and displacement abroad. But as the months wore on,
everyone got sick. They all complained of constant itchiness, most

---

[93] Many of the details in this section can be found in Casey Chalk,
     "Pearls of Greatest Price," *New Oxford Review* 84, no. 9 (Novem-
     ber 2017), https://www.newoxfordreview.org/documents/pearls-of
     -greatest-price/.

likely from scabies, a mite that burrows under the skin and itches terribly. Michael's teenage daughter developed an eye infection. His eight-year-old son's health had deteriorated so significantly that he had been released into their Filipina benefactress's care.

Michael and his family were exhausted and afraid. A Thai IDC guard had taken an unusual interest in their daughter Rochelle, personally escorting her around the compound and letting her ride his bicycle. He even once took her onto the roof alone. Nothing good was going to come from that. Then three other Pakistani Christian asylum seekers died inside the IDC, one a forty-year-old who had suspiciously died of a heart attack. Michael told me the Thai authorities refused the man's multiple requests to send him to a hospital.

Standing on the other side of this metal barrier, I beheld my wayfaring friends, hardened veterans of persecution and abuse spanning two thousand miles of Asia. Michael, with his sunken, bloodshot eyes, sought to maintain a modicum of confidence and self-respect. His elder daughter, whose penetrating hazel eyes had so often served as a testament of faith and courage amid hardship, stood back and doubled over in coughing spells. His tiny two-year-old daughter with her cute, indelible frown had spent almost as much of her life in a Thai jail as she had out of it. Could this really be a better existence than what they had fled in Karachi? Michael no longer believed it to be so.

And so, an extended cadre of concerned Christians, both in Thailand and abroad, sprang into action. Thais, Filipinos, Pakistanis, Sri Lankans, and Americans united to acquire everything necessary to assist Michael and his family with the complicated logistics of returning to Pakistan. Passports and other documentation essential for their exit were obtained. Our Catholic neighbors Jon and Crissy purchased a laptop and smartphone for them to ensure continued communication once they departed. Clothes were carefully packed into newly purchased luggage. The same neighbors, as well as my wife's parents, graciously agreed to pay for the family's plane tickets. We all threw in money to provide some additional cash for the D'Souzas to begin the process of starting over again in Pakistan.

The airfare for the flights back to Pakistan had to be paid directly to an office at the IDC. Claire carried this in cash to the IDC office on Bangkok's sky train system, the BTS. She was understandably nervous about carrying such large amounts of money on her person, especially on public transit, where pick-pocketing was common. To make matters worse, Claire had to go two or three times before she was able to pay the money to IDC officials successfully, as the "right" person at the IDC kept being out of the office, even when Claire called ahead to make sure she would be able to see him.

Once all of these logistical details were sorted out, I was as-signed the role of temporary caregiver for Michael's son, taking him from his Filipina foster mom back to the IDC, where he would spend one last night with his family before their scheduled flight. It was strange to think that a Thai immigration ministry form, probably now locked away in a forgotten filing cabinet, would forever attest to my brief guardianship of Michael's son. As the boy and I sat quietly in the detention center's lobby, I pondered: Would anybody do all of this for me? Would family, friends, and strangers around the world rally to provide vital requests in my hour of need? Could I count on people to visit me, week after week, if I were imprisoned—to pray for me, to care for me, to tell me they loved me? What compelled so many people to give so much (some families offered thousands of dol-lars) to those they hardly knew—indeed, might never know?

The Persecuted

The Gospel reading from the lectionary on the day of my last visit with Michael's family included Jesus' parables of the hidden treasure and pearl of great price: "The kingdom of heaven is like treasure hidden in a field, which a man found and covered up; then in his joy he goes and sells all that he has and buys that field. Again, the kingdom of heaven is like a merchant in search of fine pearls, who, on finding one pearl of great value, went and sold all that he had and bought it" (Matt. 13:44–46). I had always understood the man and the merchant in these corollary passages as people of faith, devout believers who had recognized the invaluable worth of reconciliation and union with God and offered everything to obtain it. Now, in light of Michael's experiences, I considered this passage afresh.

Perhaps Michael and his family were themselves the treasure hidden in the field, whom we, unknowingly blessed, had discovered buried in the dirty, crowded metropolis of Bangkok. Perhaps they were the pearls of great price, finely and painfully refined in the depths of darkness and despair that had been their lot these many years. I thought of Rochelle's haunting eyes, which pierced my soul. All of us who were united in this rescue mission had, knowingly or not, come to the same conclusion: Michael and his family were priceless, and we would do whatever was necessary to purchase their lives.

How far would a man go to save my life? In giving myself to another, I perceived more clearly the One who already had: "I am the good shepherd; I know my own and my own know me, as the Father knows me and I know the Father; and I lay down my life for the sheep" (John 10:14–15). In a lonely Thai detention center, on a hill outside Jerusalem, in a thousand other backwaters all over this aching globe, the Son of God declared in an act of unreserved assent that I, that Michael, that our families, that all of us are pearls of great price. God gave His last breath to purchase our lives for Himself.

☙

On August 3, 2017, Michael and his family departed for Karachi, back to Pakistan, back to persecution. The family was fined the equivalent of about four hundred U.S. dollars upon reentry into Pakistan — almost 40 percent of the cash we had collected for them prior to departing Thailand — supposedly for having left for so long without proper documentation. An old friend welcomed them into his home, and Michael began looking for work. A Facebook post gave an indication of his situation: "Please pray for me, for I am facing many trials in the recent months, unprecedented problems." It was unclear at the time if this meant he had already experienced renewed persecution at the hands of extremists. A later post communicated his continued commitment to Christ and His Cross: "If anybody is preaching without the Cross, he is not preaching the Gospel of Christ. There is victory in the Cross."

☙

The day Michael and his family left Bangkok was a busy one for us. I had lunch with Wilson and his family on the floor of their little two-bedroom lodging near Holy Redeemer. It was a farewell meal in another way, too, because my family was scheduled to move back to the United States the following week. I could tell Wilson's family was a bit unnerved to be losing some of their faithful advocates and benefactors. We talked, we prayed, and we took pictures to remember each other better.

Wilson's family, unlike Michael's, had successfully avoided the Thai authorities for years and had secured an integral role in the daily operations of the local Catholic parish. They often seemed despondent, but they retained hope that something, anything, might change their fortunes. After Donald Trump's election in November 2016, Wilson pulled me aside after weekday Mass. "I hear your new president is a very holy man, and that he will allow us to come to America," he said. I hesitated: "I don't think that's quite accurate."

Now, in these final hours with my friends, I sought to gather as many details as I could about their experience before returning home. Wilson told me a story I had never heard before, about a Canadian couple living in Bangkok before my family had arrived. They were Catholic and well-to-do. The husband worked for a prominent tea distributor. The couple had invested a lot of time and energy in helping Wilson and his family, much as we had done. They wrote letters to various people and organizations. They helped with English-language editing for many of the family's documents. Then, not long before my family arrived in Bangkok, they moved back to Canada. Since then, communication with the couple had dried up. Wilson sent them texts and e-mails and never received any reply. It was not hard to interpret the implicit message in Wilson's anecdote. He was concerned the same thing would happen with Claire and me; that after three years of intimate involvement in their lives, we would go back to living our suburban, white-picket-fence existence in America; that the suffering and trials experienced by Wilson's family would become distant memories.

I worried about the same thing. I had spent a summer interning at a Christian development organization in Uganda between my undergraduate and graduate school. It was a transformative experience and exposed me to the poverty of so many Africans. I developed strong friendships with many of those Ugandans, and in particular one who was about the same age as I am. A young graduate of Makerere University in Kampala, he had dreams of starting his own local development organization in his impoverished home province. I agreed to do what I could to help him realize that vision. Over the following years, I helped him found his nonprofit, sent him thousands of dollars, raised money by selling Ugandan necklaces he shipped to Virginia, and sought to acquire other American benefactors.

Yet, as the years went by, and as my professional and personal responsibilities increased, I gave less and less of my energy to my Ugandan friend. Still, he kept contacting me—calling, e-mailing, texting—expecting that I would always be his primary advocate. After Claire and I were married, we sat down to evaluate our charitable giving. My Ugandan friend was not Catholic, and we wanted to be intentional about helping Catholic organizations. I contacted him to tell him that we would be directing our charitable giving elsewhere, but also that I would send him a "golden parachute": enough money for him to cover all his expenses for a year, about four thousand U.S. dollars. Within a couple months, he was back to e-mailing, calling, and texting, asking for more money. Eventually I just began ignoring him. I still wanted to be his friend, but who wants to maintain a relationship based exclusively on being asked for cash?

With my Ugandan friend in mind, I promised Wilson that Claire and I would not abandon them, even if we were separated by thousands of miles. Wilson had never once asked me for money. He had always been genuinely interested in my family. He and his family had consistently shown grace to us—cooking us meals, assisting Claire with ensuring that she got the chalice at Mass, helping us navigate the often-complicated relationships at Holy Redeemer. Wilson and his family were true friends. Our stories were now forever linked.

The Persecuted

That evening, at dinner at a barbecue restaurant with another close friend, a South African named Daniel with whom I had played tennis every week for more than two years, I could not help but think about the whirlwind of the last twenty-four hours. The D'Souzas, who had spent eight months in a dangerous, disgusting jail, were bound for their home in Pakistan, where they would surely encounter more persecution and poverty. Wilson's family remained in a perennial limbo, able to evade Thai authorities and stay out of the IDC yet unable to bring their refugee application to a favorable conclusion that could put them on the waiting list for the West. And I was enjoying ribs and the creature comforts of expat life in Bangkok and about to return to the safety and security of the United States. None of it seemed fair.

But not every Catholic is called to endure a life of poverty —indeed, access to wealth and the right social circles can accomplish great good. Had not our ability to rally friends to give thousands of dollars for the D'Souzas proven that? St. Thomas Aquinas, in his *Summa Theologiae*, argues that in a sociopolitical system defined by distributive justice, individuals who hold "a more prominent position in the community" are entitled to "a quantity that is proportionate to the importance of the position of that part in respect of the whole." In such a position, "a person receives all the more of the common goods, according as he holds a more prominent position in the community."[94] So, according to Aquinas, there is nothing intrinsically wrong with some people having more money than others and enjoying the benefits of that wealth.

Nevertheless, in a world defined by grave inequities, where many eat and clothe themselves sumptuously while others lack

[94] St. Thomas Aquinas, *Summa Theologiae*, II-II, q. 61, art. 2.

access to potable water, such polarities cannot be easily under-stood, nor do I think Christ would intend them to be. Indeed, St. Thomas Aquinas states that "the natural division and appropria-tion of things" does not "preclude the fact that man's needs have to be remedied by means of these very things"; that "whatever certain people have in superabundance is due, by natural law, to the purpose of succoring the poor." St. Thomas cites St. Ambrose, who writes: "It is the hungry man's bread that you withhold, the naked man's cloak that you store away, the money that you bury in the earth is the price of the poor man's ransom and freedom."

As Christians, we are called, regardless of our state in life, to stand in an awkward tension, seeking to prosper, while yet remaining vigilant to answer the call of Christ, even if that call leads us into depletion, discomfort, or even death. Each one of us, says St. Thomas, "is entrusted with the stewardship of his own things, so that out of them he may come to the aid of those who are in need."[95]

Contemplating such thoughts, Claire and I, in our final week in Thailand, once more committed ourselves not only to Christ but to the peculiar mission He had given us during our three years in Bangkok. We would go back to our friends and family in America. We would refocus our efforts on our parish, our community, and on my professional success. But we would not forget our Pakistani friends.

On August 10, 2017, one week after the D'Souzas flew back to Karachi, my family flew back to the United States. Claire and I had arrived in Thailand three years earlier with a fifteen-month-old daughter. We were leaving with three children. As we made our way through Suvarnabhumi International Airport

---

[95] St. Thomas Aquinas, *Summa Theologiae*, II-II, q. 66, art. 7.

in Bangkok, I wondered where the D'Souzas had entered the airport and where they had been kept until their flight departed. Had they been the objects of any final indignities at the hands of the Thai authorities? We knew at least that they had arrived safely in Pakistan and were staying with relatives. What the future would hold for them, only God knew. I prayed for the D'Souzas and for Wilson's family one last time in this strange land before we, too, made our departure.

7

Thousands of Miles Apart

I thank my God in all my remembrance of you,
always in every prayer of mine for you all
making my prayer with joy, thankful for your partnership
in the gospel from the first day until now. And I am
sure that he who began a good work in you will bring it
to completion at the day of Jesus Christ. It is right for
me to feel thus about you all, because I hold you in my
heart, for you are all partakers with me of grace."

—Philippians 1:3–7

It was jarring how quickly my family's experiences in Thailand receded into the background once we landed in the United States in August 2017. I went from seeing Pakistani asylum seekers almost every day, to communicating with them via mobile phone messaging apps once a week, or less. I dutifully remembered to pray for them every week, but it became increasingly difficult to keep their trials in mind amid the busyness of suburban American life. I know our Pakistani friends thought a lot more about us than we did them. Wilson and Michael both sent Claire and me messages, often just to commemorate some Catholic feast day. Michael littered his Facebook page — and my Messenger phone app—with religious-themed content, sometimes in the middle of the night while I was trying to sleep.

Michael certainly needed prayers. After the D'Souzas returned to Pakistan in August 2017, Michael had difficulty finding a job.[96] He had been gone for five years. Because he feared being recognized in his old neighborhood, he moved his family to a different part of the city. More anonymity had an advantage, but it also meant that Michael could not simply go back to any of his previous employers.

In late January 2018, with funds provided by us, by Claire's parents, and by some other benefactors, Michael purchased a motorized rickshaw, or tuk-tuk, to become a taxi driver. It cost 120,000 Pakistani rupees, or about 750 U.S. dollars. We were delighted to see the picture Rosemary sent us of Michael smiling behind the wheel of the tuk-tuk. His kids, meanwhile, were back in school after their education had been interrupted by their incarceration in Bangkok. It seemed as if Michael was finally making a turn for the better, after so many hardships. Unfortunately, it was not to be.

The attack happened on St. Patrick's Day 2018 in a suburb of Karachi, North Nazimabad. Michael, driving his tuk-tuk, had just dropped off a passenger. Mullah Danish, one of the Muslim clerics

---

[96] Many of the details in this section can be found in Casey Chalk, "From a Witness in Bangkok to a Near Martyr in Karachi," *New Oxford Review*, May 2018, https://www.newoxfordreview.org/documents/from-a-witness-in-bangkok-to-a-near-martyr-in-karachi/, and Casey Chalk, "Muslim-Led Persecution Is a Global Epidemic, and It Hit My Friend Michael Again This Week," *Federalist*, March 21, 2018, https://thefederalist.com/2018/03/21/muslim-led-persecution-global-epidemic-hit-friend-michael-week/.

who had harassed Michael five years before, recognized Michael. He and three of his friends hailed Michael over. Michael, not realizing who they were, assumed they were just customers who wanted a ride. When he approached, they snarled, "We know who you are. We have been looking for you for many years." Michael still did not recognize them. They claimed to be affiliated with the Pakistani Taliban.

The men dragged Michael out of the tuk-tuk and began to beat him with a cane. They slapped his face and hit him in the head. They set fire to his vehicle. Then they saw a local police car arriving and hurriedly dispersed. The police rushed Michael to the emergency room at Abbasi Shaheed Hospital, in Karachi, his body bleeding and covered in bruises, his back marked with deep cuts. As the Lenten season approached its climax, Michael had himself become a living, physical manifestation of the suffering servant of Isaiah 53.

A police officer informed Rosemary that Michael was in the emergency room. He stayed there for four hours and then went home with his wife. Shortly thereafter, they went to report the matter at the nearest police station. The officers there listened to their account and promised to take the appropriate actions. But then they refused to give Michael and Rosemary a copy of the First Information Report, or FIR. They also declared they would not officially file the incident unless the D'Souzas gave the officers 75,000 Pakistani rupees, about 470 U.S. dollars. Michael and Rosemary did not have that kind of money. Indeed, they had just lost their only source of income.

The day after the assault, Rosemary sent us photos and videos of Michael. They were sobering. He lay in a bed, looking half-dead, bruises all over his body, blood visible on gauze bandages covering his forehead and arm. A video showed stripes across his back and Michael screaming in pain while a family member applied various medicines to the wounds.

Halfway around the world, in Virginia, it snowed half a foot, and I was unable to go to work. Rosemary called while I was shoveling snow. She was noticeably disturbed. She passed the phone to Michael. He sounded terrible. Words came slowly and confusedly from a man who usually spoke in rapid-fire utterances. He told me they needed to leave Pakistan. He seemed like a broken man.

Leaving was certainly one option. But I thought Michael should give the tuk-tuk one more try—and maybe grow a long, bushy beard to fit in with the Muslim majority. In the hope of raising awareness about his plight, I wrote an article about the attack on Michael for the *Federalist*, an online conservative magazine. One of the website's editors asked me if there was a way for readers to send money to Michael's family, perhaps via a GoFundMe site.

My wife, who is tech-savvy, immediately set to work on the GoFundMe site and uploaded a video of Michael to YouTube.[97] We set our fundraising goal at five thousand dollars, which we estimated would cover a replacement tuk-tuk, medical expenses, and other financial needs while Michael recovered from his injuries. If the videos Rosemary had sent us were any indication, Michael would likely be physically incapable of working for weeks, if not months. Quite frankly, we did not really think that our goal would be reached. But the response was startling: within three days, contributions exceeded that goal by hundreds of dollars, much

[97] Claire C., "Please Help Persecuted Pakistani Christian Michael DSouza and Family," YouTube video, 4:45, January 14, 2019, https://www.youtube.com/watch?v=AMN4ynojRPs&feature=youtu.be&fbclid=IwAR2wx0zkFrOJx6lBCOoX.g4Jru TEMWvFN5mRk-yaniwzr8HslZQINONlqxVU.

of the money coming from complete strangers who had read my article in the *Federalist*. Even the editor who suggested the idea sent us some money. We praised God for His faithfulness, and my wife wired the money to Karachi.

The D'Souzas' Filipina benefactress urged Michael to take his family and flee to Europe. In 2015, German chancellor Angela Merkel had welcomed in more than one million migrants, both as a humanitarian gesture and as a way to fill a need for working-class labor.[98] With the money my wife had just sent them from our fundraising campaign, the D'Souzas now had the means for such a transcontinental escape. I was skeptical of the idea, given the tremendous risks. But I would have understood if they had pursued this plan. The day before the attack on Michael, the *Washington Post* had published an article by veteran reporter and Afghanistan-Pakistan bureau chief Pamela Constable on the persecution of Christians in Pakistan. The article mentioned the "growing reach and aggressiveness of Pakistan's once-obscure anti-blasphemy movement, which has gained wide support since staging a three-week protest outside the capital, Islamabad, in November [2017]."[99]

While Constable's picture of prejudice and violence against Pakistani Christians was welcome, her implication that it was

---

[98] Judith Vonberg, "Why Angela Merkel Is No Longer the 'Refugee Chancellor,'" CNN, July 6, 2018, https://www.cnn.com /2018/07/06/europe/angela-merkel-migration-germany-intl/ index.html.

[99] Pamela Constable, "Christians Come Under Threat in Pakistan: 'No One Accused of Blasphemy Is Ever Safe,'" *Washington Post*, March 16, 2018, https://www.washingtonpost.com/world/ asia_pacific/christians-come-under-threat-in-pakistan-no-one-accused-of-blasphemy-is-ever-safe/2018/03/15/d5f88f46-232b-11e8-946c-9420060cb7bd_story.html.

a relatively new phenomenon seemed grossly out of step with circumstances on the ground. Christians had increasingly become the target of Muslim reprisals since the 1990s. And the violence aside, Pakistani Christians endured many other sociocultural and economic prejudices in their land of origin. Most Christians worked menial jobs at below subsistence wages, as evidenced by Michael's difficulties finding work upon his return to Pakistan in 2017.

The future was unclear for Michael and his family. They were grateful for the generous donations made on their behalf as Lenten alms from their five fellow parishioners on the other side of the world. Yet Michael's family was worn down, with few options. Every choice available to them carried risk. I hoped that my article in the *Federalist*, a publication that at the time had some influence in the corridors of power in Washington, D.C., might pique the interest of some politician or government official with the power to put Michael and his family on a one-way flight to the United States. But the chance of that was remote. As with so many of life's grave problems, we were left to pray.

After the physical assault, Michael spent the next few months in recovery, both at a hospital and in his home.[100] Much of the money my wife raised on his behalf went toward his medical expenses. I again urged Michael to grow a long beard and wear clothes like the Muslims who attacked him. Blending in and

---

[100] Many of the details in this section can be found in Casey Chalk, "Learning the Meaning of Longsuffering," *New Oxford Review* (January–February 2019), https://www.newoxfordreview.org/documents/learning-the-meaning-of-longsuffering/.

apostasy are two entirely different things; there was no reason to draw attention to himself in a city full of men eager to make examples of Christians. We heard little from Michael and Rosemary for several months.

But in July 2018, they sent us a message saying that they were no longer in Pakistan. They were afraid for their lives and wanted to try applying for asylum again. They first tried to get a visa to fly to Azerbaijan. They had heard that they needed only to show a copy of their bank statement to apply for a visa (other countries required a letter of employment as well). At first, things seemed promising. They were granted a visa to go to Azerbaijan and arrived in Baku, the capital, on June 8, 2018. But at the UNHCR office in Azerbaijan, they met a man named Namee, who told them that they were wasting their time trying to apply for asylum in Azerbaijan. Instead, the shady individual suggested they could pay one of his family members to get them into majority-Catholic and EU-member Poland. He also promised them a job and a house in Poland. The journey, said Namee, would take them to the EU by way of Moscow.

I was highly suspicious. Poland, along with several other Eastern European countries, had rebuffed the liberal immigration policies of the EU, and specifically its neighbor Germany.[101] Even if Michael's family were persecuted Catholics, would Poland be willing to take them in? It seemed a foolhardy mission.

But Michael paid the man 3,500 U.S. dollars, some of which came directly from the rest of the GoFundMe money. The

[101] Jonas Ekblom, "Poland, Hungary Broke EU Laws by Refusing to Host Migrants: Court Adviser," Reuters, October 31, 2019, https://www.reuters.com/article/us-europe-migration-court/poland-hungary-broke-eu-laws-by-refusing-to-host-migrants-court-adviser-idUSKBN1XA1S5.

The Persecuted

D'Souzas left Azerbaijan on June 28, 2018, and flew to Russia. Namee had given the family FIFA World Cup Fan identification cards to travel in Russia without a visa, as the 2018 World Cup was in Russia. On July 1, 2018, the family traveled to Belarus by train, accompanied by Namee. On July 4, 2018, while in Minsk, Namee bought the family tickets for a train to Poland, and then he left the family to go alone.

At the Polish border, customs officials checked their passports and declared they could not travel into Poland without a visa, for which they would have to apply in Pakistan.

To make matters worse, a Polish customs official marked their passports to show they had tried to enter the country illegally. Polish authorities forced them onto a train back to Russia, where the family returned on July 6, 2018. In Russia, police told them that if they did not go back to Pakistan, they would be sent to prison.

Needless to say, the smuggler who had promised them a new life had disappeared along with the remainder of their money, which he had claimed would be used to fund their new life in Poland. Once more, their Filippina benefactress came to the rescue and helped pay to get them back to Pakistan, the only country they could legally enter and avoid being imprisoned indefinitely. They returned to Pakistan on July 11, 2018. The whole ordeal was over in a little over one month.

I was livid. My wife had raised thousands of dollars to pay for Michael's medical expenses and repair his tuk-tuk or purchase a new one. Much of the money had come from family and friends and even some of my professional contacts in the media and publishing world. The money had evaporated, squandered on a reckless, ill-conceived scheme. Of course, once my wife wired the money, it was Michael's to do with as he pleased. But it would be impossible to make another round of financial requests. When Michael and Rosemary requested that we pursue more fundraising, we flatly refused.

This, I had to admit, was the cold, hard reality of trying to help persecuted Pakistani Christians, especially when separated by thousands of miles and a ten-hour time difference. Michael was, and always will be, my friend. But much will always divide us. His English is adequate but rudimentary; his education minimal; his brand of Catholicism is fervent and pious but emotive, charismatic, and hyper-focused on the supernatural in a way that sometimes left me incredulous. I could not expect him to think or act like me. But I was deeply frustrated by his behavior.

⸙

Nevertheless, around the same time Michael and his family made their attempted escape to Europe, some positive developments occurred in the United States. Pieter Vree, editor of *New Oxford Review*, which had published several of my articles on the asylum-seeker crisis in Bangkok, contacted the office of New Jersey Republican congressman Chris Smith regarding the D'Souzas. Fr. Peter M. J. Stravinskas, editor of the *Catholic Response*, had recommended Congressman Smith as an advocate of persecuted Christians around the world. Smith's office, in turn, relayed Michael's case to the Jubilee Campaign, a nonprofit organization that promotes the human rights and religious liberty of ethnic and religious minorities in countries such as Pakistan. Jubilee contacted us, expressed interest in Michael's case, and requested all relevant information and documents that we had available. Jubilee also told us that they were willing to assist with getting his refugee application reopened with the UNHCR.

The Persecuted

Claire and I were quite excited by this news. But we had no idea how much labor would be required of us. In September 2018, Jubilee informed us that Michael's old UNHCR refugee application was so terribly written — incorrect use of tense and pronouns, among other things —that it was impossible to understand. Indeed, a Jubilee staff member had spent an hour and a half on the phone with Michael, but Michael's English (and accent) was so difficult to understand that the staff member was able to acquire the appropriate level of detail and clarity on only one incident from Michael's application. For any action to be taken, Michael's story would have to be completely rewritten and expanded all the way back to the beginning in 2005. Now we understood why the UNHCR had so often required Urdu interpreters for their interviews with Pakistani asylum-seekers in Bangkok.

Jubilee said that for progress to be made, we would have to go through the entire application systematically, gathering and recording all details from Michael and his family. Jubilee presumed it would be faster for Claire and me to do this than for them to do it, since we were more familiar with the complexity of their case. Thus began the next chapter in our attempt to assist this impoverished, persecuted Pakistani Catholic family.

Claire took over this slow, arduous process, identifying fifteen events that needed to be recorded. Whenever she could steal away from family responsibilities, she would read through the account of an event from Michael's application and then compare it with a letter from Michael's parish priest in Pakistan, as well as the information gathered from my previous interviews with him. Then she would draft several numbered questions and e-mail them to Michael in Pakistan. She could manage to discuss only one incident at a time, as details would get confused because of

Michael's limited command of English grammar. This would be followed by back-and-forth e-mails and text messages with Rosemary for further clarification. Verb tenses and prepositions were especially difficult for the D'Souzas. One time, Claire creatively drew cartoons to clarify an incident and then recorded a video of herself explaining the cartoons to Michael to ensure she had properly interpreted his story.

Slowly, Claire illuminated what Michael's family had suffered over the past fourteen years. Many details of their family story—the kidnappings of Michael's and Rosemary's sisters, for example—I had never heard before. After three months, Claire had rewritten all the requisite information.

Staff from the Jubilee Campaign reviewed Claire's documentation and then asked her to schedule a meeting with Ann Buwalda, Jubilee's executive director. Things finally seemed to be progressing. During that meeting on Presidents' Day 2019, Buwalda and a staff member mentioned someone else who might be able to assist with Michael's situation, which they deemed somewhat unusual. Buwalda explained that there was a very small chance that with the support of Congressman Smith's office, Michael could submit a humanitarian-aid application to the U.S. Government for a visa to come to the United States in order to apply for asylum with the UNHCR.[102] If Michael's asylum application were accepted, his family would be able to join him in the United States within a few months.

---

[102] Details on this process can be found in "Humanitarian or Significant Public Benefit Parole for Individuals Outside the United States," U.S. Citizenship and Immigration Services, https://www.uscis.gov/humanitarian/humanitarian-or-significant-public-benefit-parole-individuals-outside-united-states.

There was more good news. Buwalda also asked for permission to use Michael's case as an example of global persecution of Christians during a hearing before a congressional subcommittee. We were elated. Buwalda asked for affidavits from all U.S. citizens that knew Michael personally. Between Claire and me, Claire's parents, and our neighbors from Bangkok who had helped fund the D'Souzas' flights back to Pakistan, we were able to submit six affidavits. Not long afterward, Claire received an e-mail from Jubilee:

> We have been in touch with Congressman Smith's office regarding testifying to Congress on the refugee situation in Thailand since last Fall and we have been asked to testify, drawing attention to particular cases as an illustrative example of the obstacles faced by religious minorities in Pakistan and elsewhere. If given the opportunity, we will be highlighting the D'Souza family's case during our testimony!

This was the kind of exposure we had long prayed for, the kind that might generate enough high-profile interest to finally get Michael and his family out of Pakistan.

Meanwhile, the D'Souzas spent their days locked in their home in Karachi. Michael, afraid for his personal safety, refused to look for alternative employment. The D'Souzas were scared even to send their three children to school. They invited a teacher to come to the house to tutor their children, though Muslim neighbors confronted the instructor and discouraged her from visiting any Christian families. My wife and some of our extended family continued to send them a small amount of money periodically, though we knew it was not nearly enough to pay their basic expenses. Meanwhile, Michael and his family, once again, waited.

The word *long-suffering* is often used in Scripture. And indeed, the long-suffering of Michael and his family impacted all of us. In the union of the Mystical Body of Christ, we were able to unite our prayers and our efforts in Washington. This, it seemed, is what St. Paul had in mind when he wrote, "Now I rejoice in my sufferings for your sake, and in my flesh I complete what is lacking in Christ's afflictions for the sake of his body, that is, the church" (Col. 1:24).

Our Lord has offered us—weak, frail, selfish, and easily distracted—an opportunity to participate in His redemptive work on Earth. Thus, every prayerful effort we made on behalf of Michael and his family worked in small, imperceptible ways to build and bless Christ's Body. So we labored on, praying that someday we would have a far greater story to tell.

8

Rising Fears, Political and Bureaucratic Frustrations

Behold, I send you out as sheep in the midst of wolves; so be wise as serpents and innocent as doves. Beware of men; for they will deliver you up to councils, and flog you in their synagogues, and you will be dragged before governors and kings for my sake, to bear testimony before them and the Gentiles. When they deliver you up, do not be anxious how you are to speak or what you are to say; for what you are to say will be given to you in that hour; for it is not you who speak, but the Spirit of your Father speaking through you. . . . And you will be hated by all for my name's sake. But he who endures to the end will be saved.

—Matthew 10:16–22

On October 31, 2018, Asia Bibi, the Pakistani Christian accused of blasphemy, was acquitted by the Supreme Court of Pakistan because of "material contradictions and inconsistent statements of the witnesses."[103] As I've noted, her story is painfully similar

[103] Many of the details in this section can be found in Casey Chalk, "Christian Persecution on the Rise as 7 Are Martyred in Egypt," *Aleteia*, November 7, 2018, https://aleteia.org/2018/11/07/christian-persecution-on-the-rise-as-7-are-martyred-in-egypt/.

to that of Wilson's and Michael's families: Bibi had been accused of blasphemy in June 2009 after an argument with Muslim coworkers while harvesting berries. Because Bibi was Christian, her accusers refused to drink from a bucket of water she had touched.[104]

Among the extremist Muslim leaders opposed to Bibi's exoneration was Pakistani cleric Maulana Sami-ul-Haq, known as the father of the Taliban. But on November 2, Haq was assassinated by unknown assailants in Rawalpindi, Pakistan.[105] Haq had intended to join national protests against the acquittal of Asia Bibi in Islamabad, but he was prohibited because of a road blockage, according to a bodyguard.[106] Following the assassination, the

---

[104] In her memoir *Free at Last*, Bibi explains that "the Islamists and their influence are terrible because everybody fears them—even the ministers and the president. Everyone feels helpless because the Islamists aren't afraid to lay down bombs or ally with the Taliban to kill others and themselves in Allah's name. In fact, I think the judges who sentenced me to death in the Nankana Court and High Court of Lahore must have been scared of them too." See Bibi and Tollet, *Free at Last*, 46.

[105] "Maulana Samiul Haq Assassinated at His Home in Rawalpindi," Geo News, November 2, 2018, https://www.geo.tv/latest/217054-maulana-samiul-haq-killed-in-targetted-attack-in-rawalpindi, and "Maulana Samiul Haq Assassinated at Rawalpindi Residence," *Dawn*, November 2, 2018, https://www.dawn.com/news/1443118/maulana-samiul-haq-assassinated-in-rawalpindi.

[106] "Slain Maulana Samiul Haq Laid to Rest in Darul Uloom Haqqania," *News International*, November 3, 2018, https://www.thenews.com.pk/latest/389181-funeral-prayers-for-maulana-samiul-haq-offered-in-akora-khattak, and Jibran Ahmed and Asif Shahzad, "'Father of Taliban' Mullah Sami ul-Haq killed in Pakistan: Deputy," Reuters, November 2, 2018, https://www.reuters.com/article/us-pakistan-cleric-taliban/father-of-taliban-mullah-sami-ul-haq-killed-in-pakistani-city-deputy-idUSKCN1N71U3.

government of the Pakistani province of Khyber Pakhtunkhwa declared a day of mourning. Members of Haq's party pinned his murder on "enemies of Islam," leading many Pakistani Christians to fear that reprisals would target their communities. Indeed, Islamist groups in the streets reportedly chanted slogans of "Death to Asia Bibi, death to blasphemers."[107]

Both Wilson and Michael contacted me after the Asia Bibi ruling and the assassination of Maulana Sami-ul-Haq. Wilson, still in Bangkok, sent me several videos that showed extremist Muslim clerics in Pakistan condemning the decision and calling on Pakistani Muslims to avenge this supposed insult to their faith. Michael wrote to us from Karachi and explained that the situation for Pakistani Christians was "very bad" and that some Muslims were grabbing passersby on the streets and asking them if they were Christians.

The October and November events reinvigorated our efforts to bring Michael's plight to the attention of American officials. The longer we labored, the more we came to understand how easy it was for Michael to be lost among the thousands of other cases brought before humanitarian organizations and the U.S. government. Was his story unique and compelling enough to warrant special attention? Yet we continued to pray and hope.

☞

On February 26, 2019, our prayers for progress in the D'Souza case were answered. Ann Buwalda of the Jubilee Campaign was

---

[107] Shamil Shams, "Pakistan Dangles between Hope and Despair over Minority Rights," DW, December 24, 2018, https://www.dw.com/en/pakistan-dangles-between-hope-and-despair-over-minority-rights/a-46854397.

invited to speak to the U.S. House Foreign Affairs Subcommittee on Africa, Global Health, Global Human Rights and International Organizations. She submitted to the subcommittee written testimony that included several examples of religious persecution around the world. The very first case she cited was the D'Souzas', to which she devoted more than a page. Buwalda also cited a report by Amnesty International (AI), which discussed the various and sundry challenges faced by asylum seekers such as Michael's family:

> Limited employment prospects, trouble accessing medical care and educational opportunities, financial stresses, self-imposed restrictions on movement and social interactions, and the constant fear of arrest. Refugees and asylum-seekers arrested for immigration violations may face prolonged and indefinite detention in appalling conditions in IDCs.... UN human rights bodies, UNHCR and civil society organizations have repeatedly raised concerns about the prolonged detention of refugees and asylum-seekers, the poor conditions in IDCs, and the impact of these factors on the physical, psychological and social wellbeing of those seeking protection in Thailand.... Given the stark realities of detention and refugee life in Thailand, some refugees and asylum-seekers make the difficult decision to return to their home countries and face the dangers and hardships that caused them to seek protection abroad.[108]

---

[108] Amnesty International, *Between a Rock and a Hard Place: Thailand's Refugee Policies and Violations of the Principle of NonRefoulement* (London: Amnesty International, 2017), 41–42. Ann Buwalda's testimony may be found at the following link: https://

Buwalda's testimony highlighted the persecution Michael had experienced after his return to Pakistan, including his being attacked by Islamic extremists and the destruction of his tuk-tuk:

> Sadly, Mr. D'Souza's return to Pakistan confirmed the reasons why he should have been granted his refugee status determination by the UNHCR. Those whom he feared, found and bludgeoned him just as they had threatened to do years earlier. Although refugees may appear to "voluntarily" self-deport, serious questions arise as to whether those deportations are truly "voluntary" or, due to the overwhelming economic, emotional, and physical difficulties for refugees in Thailand, whether the refugees are insidiously, indirectly coerced to deport. The AI report states, "refoulement [forceable deportment] need not be accomplished using physical coercion". International law also prohibits "constructive" refoulement, which occurs when states use indirect means to coerce the return of individuals to situations where they are likely to face human rights violations. UNHCR's "Handbook on Voluntary Repatriation" states, "The principle of voluntariness is the cornerstone of international protection with respect to the return of refugees". While a number of factors, including the economic, social and cultural pressures may affect whether a return is voluntary, lack of legal status and indefinite confinement can be chief drivers in an involuntary decision to return to one's country of origin.[109]

---

files.constantcontact.com/c5fd56509e/65cfeceb-8f75-4690-bf45-e5f4923ec437.pdf.

[109] Ann Buwalda, written testimony submitted to the House Foreign Affairs Subcommittee on Africa, Global Health, Global

The Persecuted

We were thrilled to see Michael's case so prominently featured in Jubilee's written testimony. But the subcommittee hearing itself was quickly sidetracked as subcommittee members aired various personal political grievances, many of which were only tangentially related to the topic at hand.[110] Rep. Karen Bass of California, the Democrat who chaired the subcommittee, complained about President Trump's Executive Order 13769, titled "Protecting the Nation from Foreign Terrorist Entry into the United States," which had been politically labeled a "Muslim ban" by Trump's detractors. Democrat Rep. Ilhan Omar of Minnesota, in turn, portrayed Muslim refugees as facing unfair discrimination, even as she downplayed the deplorable treatment of Christians and other religious minorities in the Muslim world.

But thankfully, New Jersey Rep. Chris Smith did raise Michael's case during the hearing and called the current situation in Thailand for persecuted Christians "appalling." He referred, with notable anger in his voice, to the travesty of Michael's being attacked in Pakistan, fleeing to Thailand, and then being attacked again upon his return. He also mentioned that Michael's and Rosemary's sisters were "beaten" by Muslim extremists in Pakistan, though the reality was quite a bit graver: they were beaten, kidnapped, forcibly converted to Islam, coerced into marrying Muslim men, and never heard from again.

Human Rights, and International Organizations for the hearing record on "A Global Crisis: Refugees, Migrants and Asylum Seekers," February 26, 2019, https://files.constantcontact.com/c5fd56509e/65cfeceb-8f75-4690-bf45-e5f4923ec437.pdf.

[110] See House Foreign Affairs Committee, "02.26.19 Subcommittee Hearing: A Global Crisis: Refugees, Migrants and Asylum Seekers," YouTube video, 2:59:22, February 26, 2019, youtube.com/watch?v=cC1jO2UQQkk.

Rep. Smith, also to his credit, expressed a desire to hold the UNHCR more accountable for the low approval rate of Pakistani Christians for refugee status and asked for advice from the panel. Buwalda, in her response to Smith, discussed the UNHCR's "unbalanced burden of proof" toward asylum seekers as well as an institutional "basic skepticism" toward Pakistani asylum seekers. She also noted that from 2016 to 2017, the years Claire and I had spent in Bangkok, the UNHCR had sought to rush backlogged cases through. "The fastest way to do that," explained Buwalda, "is to deny them." Moreover, many of these rejections included an "adverse credibility claim," meaning that the adjudicator determined that the applicant was lying. This, added Buwalda, made appeals almost impossible. The UNHCR, readers will remember, had expressed skepticism seemingly from the beginning about the testimonies of members of both Wilson's and Michael's families.

The summary of the subcommittee hearing on Jubilee's website was published two days after the hearing.[111] It reads, in part: "Buwalda featured the case of Michael D'Souza as a clear example of the misapplication of asylum adjudication standards. He was denied asylum by the UNHCR in Bangkok, resulting in his placement in the deplorable conditions of the Thai immigration detention facility." Jubilee and Buwalda had worked very hard to help profile the D'Souza's case in the halls of America's highest legislative body.

Afterward, Rep. Smith's office, again much to his credit, agreed to write a letter formally sponsoring Michael and his family for refugee status in the United States. This letter would

[111] "Ann Buwalda's Testimony before Congressional Subcomittee," Jubilee Campaign USA, February 28, 2019, http://jubileecampaign.org/subcommittee/.

be delivered to Jubilee, and Jubilee would submit a request to the U.S. Department of State on behalf of the D'Souzas for a humanitarian visa. The sponsorship of Smith's office would significantly increase the likelihood of the visa's being issued. If it was approved, Michael would first come over by himself for four to six weeks to await designation as an asylum seeker. Once that happened, the rest of the family would be allowed to join him. They would then apply for full refugee status with the UNHCR while residing in the United States.

In March and April 2019, Jubilee coordinated with Claire to complete the humanitarian-aid application. Claire, in turn, worked with Michael, and we paid for him to send the documents back to the United States. In May, Claire's parents completed an I-134 form and added that to Michael's not-yet-submitted application. The I-134 stated that if Michael was resettled in the United States, Claire's parents were willing to take on the financial responsibility of providing for Michael, and potentially his entire family, until he received a work permit, which could take months, and to be sued if Michael applied for any public financial aid while waiting for his permit.[112]

At the end of May, Claire checked with Jubilee and learned that they were still waiting on Rep. Smith's office. At the end of June, Claire contacted the attorney in Rep. Smith's office who was responsible for the sponsorship letter. He said he would hope to get it back to us within the week.

---

[112] A U.S. Department of State employee told me that the I-134 is a "joke" that is rarely, if ever, used. Indeed, Chinese-language newspapers would advertise their services as a sponsor, for a fee. Eventually the U.S. government started keeping track of social security numbers of sponsors, so that they could not sponsor more people than their declared income permits.

While we waited, my wife and I reached out to our own representative, Democrat Gerald "Gerry" Connolly of Virginia. She finally got hold of one of Connolly's staffers, who expressed surprise that no one had returned our calls. "We'll definitely get back to you," she promised. We never heard back. When my wife finally complained, the congressman's staffer apologized profusely, saying this was "unprecedented." The D'Souzas were no longer being squeezed solely by the vise of Islamic extremism. Their fate was now entangled in the U.S. federal bureaucracy.

The next few months brought more of the same. Family friends contacted their congressmen without any success. Claire's patience was increasingly spent. She began having more frank conversations with Rep. Smith's attorney on the phone. The attorney explained that many people falsely believed that all they needed was that reference letter from the congressman. In truth, it was basically useless with the U.S. Citizenship and Immigration Services (USCIS) unless there was much more political work (i.e., securing other politicians' support) done beforehand. He asked for Claire's patience and promised that he would keep Michael in mind and try to advance his case whenever possible. The attorney thought there would be little chance for Michael's application without this.

As the process stalled, the signatures on Michael's humanitarian-aid application expired. We had to get a new set of signatures from Michael sent from Pakistan. My wife and I were increasingly frustrated. We did not fault Rep. Smith or his office; we were not even his constituents. How many other people, especially knowing that Rep. Smith possesses a gracious, listening ear, were constantly petitioning his office? Yet we felt that God had placed the D'Souzas in our lives purposefully and that we had a duty to advocate for them.

The Persecuted

As for the D'Souzas, life continued much the same through most of 2019. Over the summer, they made arrangements for their two younger children to leave the house to attend a nearby school. Michael and Rosemary occasionally slipped out at night to purchase groceries and other necessities. Otherwise, it was a deadening existence, punctuated by the kinds of fearful moments that steal sleep from the already weary.

On August 29, 2019, we received a haunting message from Michael and Rosemary.[113] They had seen Mullah Danish walking in the alley next to their home. They texted us a photo of Danish from behind, an ominous specter of what otherwise appeared to be the back of an anonymous man, but whom the D'Souzas assured us was indeed Danish.

Danish's presence in their neighborhood on the outskirts of Karachi, Pakistan, was alarming. He had been hounding the D'Souzas since 2005. Thankfully, Michael and Rosemary didn't think that the mullah knew the D'Souzas lived there. But the whole family was understandably terrified.

Michael and Rosemary begged my wife and me to help get them and their children out of Pakistan as quickly as possible.

We started to wonder if we should try to push Michael's application through without further political support. Given the heightened concerns raised by Mullah Danish's presence, that seemed as if it might be a better option. We were afraid that Michael might be killed before we even submitted the application, and Michael seemed to be thinking along similar lines.

---

[113] Many of the details in this section can be found in Casey Chalk, "In Bureaucracy's Grip," *New Oxford Review* (November 2019), https://www.newoxfordreview.org/documents/in-bureaucracys -grip/.

In October 2019, he asked for our help to go back to Thailand. Michael had heard that there was a sympathetic priest in Thailand who was helping Pakistanis relocate to Canada. Claire reminded him that, because of his overstay last time, the country's authorities had barred him from reentering for ten years. If Michael attempted to go back, he would likely be put directly into the IDC.

Around that same time, Claire's parents contacted their congresswoman, Democrat Lucy Kay McBath. Quite to our surprise, they received a call back. We thought Rep. McBath's position on the House Judiciary Committee might help Michael, so we delayed the application in hopes of securing another support letter. Then we learned that the application would have to be submitted *before* Rep. McBath could formally support the application. This put us in the awkward position of choosing between Rep. Smith and Rep. McBath. Claire consulted Rep. Smith's attorney, who explained that he was making progress and that Rep. Smith's seniority would be helpful.

Months later, in early 2020, Smith's attorney told Claire that given the new political climate's skepticism toward immigration, Michael's application had no chance unless the right person was willing to walk the application through USCIS. The attorney promised he was keeping Michael in mind and advancing his case whenever possible.

Then, in March 2020, the coronavirus quarantines began in Virginia. Claire reached out to Ann Buwalda. All the timelines that she had originally given Claire had to be extended. Applications that usually required weeks to be processed had been waiting for months. Alarmingly, Buwalda expected it could take years, rather than months, to obtain work permits, which meant that even if the D'Souzas were able to emigrate to America, Claire's parents could be financially responsible for them for *years* instead of months.

The Persecuted

When the Trump administration announced further limits on immigration, Claire relayed the news to Rosemary, explaining that recent changes in U.S. immigration policy, coupled with the coronavirus, might permanently affect their chances of resettlement in America. She made it clear that we were not going to submit the application anytime soon. Though we had no wish to encourage them to pursue riskier options, we wanted to make clear that if, by some extraordinary chance, another opportunity to leave Pakistan presented itself, they should consider prioritizing that over our stalled efforts.

⌒

Meanwhile, Michael related to me that embassies and consulates in Pakistan—when they weren't closed because of the coronavirus—were giving priority to Muslim applicants, making his prospects even more remote. But at least the need to wear a mask in public served as a useful disguise. And the family continued to survive. They traveled on Sunday to their Catholic parish, Christ the King; and Michael watched daily Mass on the laptop we provided him with when he departed Thailand. However, Michael's younger children were attending a Muslim school where they were exposed to frequent and aggressive Muslim proselytizing; and when Rochelle went out in public, young men, including some riding motorbikes, would try to touch her as she walked by. Michael was very afraid that Rochelle would be forced into a marriage. Indeed, in April 2020, a fourteen-year-old altar girl in Karachi was abducted and impressed into a marriage with a Muslim man before escaping in August.[114]

---

[114] Kamram Chaudry, "Catholic Altar Girl in Hiding in Pakistan After Escaping Abductor," UCA News, August 31, 2020, https://

⌒

St. Paul writes that "hope does not disappoint us, because God's love has been poured into our hearts through the Holy Spirit who has been given to us" (Rom. 5:5). Elsewhere in the Bible we read, "Let us hold fast the confession of our hope without wavering, for he who promised is faithful" (Heb. 10:23).

The theological virtue of hope has as its object God Himself, Creator of the universe and Sustainer of all being. Yet hope is more than an abstract intellectual exercise. We hope in a God who has proved Himself throughout Scripture and history; who rose from the dead, as He said He would, after three days; who has promised, "I am with you always, to the close of the age" (Matt. 28:20). And He has been with us, despite the labors of many a strong man to wipe Him and His memory off the face of the earth. If our hope is in Christ, however desperate the circumstances, our hope is not in vain.

The D'Souzas future is still highly uncertain. But there is always hope. We had thought, as 2019 ended, that we might be welcoming Michael and his family to the United States by Christmas, even knowing that our hopes, and prayers, are often restricted by our own limited view of what God might do. Certainly, my own prayers for the D'Souzas often became embarrassingly monotonous and predictable, perhaps because I had grown tired of the pain stemming from God's perceived silence. Yet such seemingly intractable problems reminded me even more of the need to recommit to a more diligent form of supplication. As the next chapter shows, boldly entreating the halls of Heaven can have dramatic results.

---

www.ucanews.com/news/catholic-altar-girl-in-hiding-in-pakistan-after-escaping-abductor/89343#.

9

Exciting News

And this is the confidence which we have in him,
that if we ask anything according to his will he hears us.

—1 John 5:14

Wilson's family prayed without ceasing.[115] For years, their supplications were brought before the altar of God in far-flung cities such as Karachi and Bangkok, their pious petitions wedded to bitter weeping. And then, after many trials and tears, when their story seemed all but over and their supplications forgotten, God answered, as "deep calls to deep at the thunder of thy cataracts" (Ps. 42:7).

It was early November 2019 when we got an unexpected message from Wilson and his wife, Maryam. They had applied to the Italian embassy in Bangkok for humanitarian sponsorship and had received a Schengen visa, which allows people to travel to more than twenty countries in Europe. A wealthy Pakistani

---

[115] Many of the details in this section can be found in Casey Chalk, "They Prayed without Ceasing," *Crisis Magazine*, December 9, 2019, https://www.crisismagazine.com/2019/they-prayed-without -ceasing.

businessman in Holland—where Wilson's brother had lived as a placed refugee for several years—had then sponsored them for resettlement. But they needed money, lots of it, to pay for plane tickets. We were a bit confused by how Wilson and his family had acquired these documents and what exactly they meant.[116] Moreover, even if we could get them the money for international airfare, would the Thai authorities allow them to leave without a huge fine when they had overstayed their visas by years? Yet we trusted Wilson enough to act quickly to provide assistance. My wife, the ever-shrewd administrator, began contacting people to raise the necessary funds. Once more, she succeeded, petitioning family and friends for aid to help Wilson's family in their hour of need.

Yet a new complication arose: Claire was not able to wire them the money because the deadline was short and wiring money internationally from the United States to Thailand could take two weeks or more. Furthermore, no one in Wilson's family had a bank account in Thailand, and no one would be able to open one in that country because of laws governing visa requirements for bank accounts within Thailand. Western Union was a possible, faster alternative, but the exchange rate was frustratingly high compared with the bank-to-bank rate. We were also concerned about Wilson walking out of a Western Union office with thousands of dollars' worth of Thai currency on his person.

Wilson suggested wiring the money to a trusted friend of his family. But trusted or not, we were afraid that several thousand dollars might be too tempting for anyone's friend. So, we decided

---

[116] I feared what I might learn if I was too insistent in querying Wilson regarding what had happened. Wilson, for his sake, was not particularly forthcoming with details.

to pay the exorbitant Western Union rate. Claire sent $1,000 the first day, in early November, waited for a confirmation that Wilson picked up the money successfully, and then sent another cash transfer of $2,530 a couple of days later. We prayed that no pickpockets or enterprising criminals would intercept Wilson on his journey home. On November 8, some of our fears were relieved when Wilson sent Claire a text message with a picture of their airline tickets. They were scheduled to leave Bangkok on November 18.

Within a week of receiving his initial request, I received the following message from Wilson:

> Good morning. I am very glad to be informing you that by the grace of God my wife and kids left for Amsterdam. And it's all happened because of your prayers and support. Thank you so much for all your help and support. May God bless you more and more.

But it was not our prayers but theirs; not my support but that of my friends and family. Wilson also forwarded to us a photo of his wife and three children, with several members of their extended family, taken at the airport upon their arrival in the Netherlands. They immediately settled in a refugee camp, where they had to stay temporarily before moving into permanent housing.

Unfortunately, much work remained to be done. Wilson himself, and many of his family members, were still in Thailand. He had chosen to stay behind in Bangkok in order to help everyone else, especially his elderly parents, get the requisite paperwork to travel to Europe. He told me that he hoped the process would take only two or three months. We committed to pray for them, as well as for Wilson's family in Holland, that they might find work and a community in which to worship.

The Persecuted

"He who prays most receives most," said St. Alphonsus Liguori.[117] I confess that often (in my sin and doubt) I do not act as if I believe those words. Yet the story of Wilson and his family showed me how God does answer. This was not just a story about a devout, poor Catholic family who kept the faith. It was also about my wife, Claire, a busy mother of three in Virginia who made the continued, conscious effort to remain engaged in the lives of people halfway around the world. In the process, she was given the grace to participate in God's great plans.

It was also a story about one of my closest friends—a single, middle-aged, devout Catholic with a good job but frequent doubts about his purpose in life. While he worked in a profession that he loved and that engaged his imagination, he constantly questioned his calling, wondering whether his frustrations in finding a wife suggested that he should pursue a religious vocation. Yet it was my friend, always so conservative and discerning with his finances, who was positioned to be used by God to help Wilson's family. My friend personally donated thousands of his hard-earned dollars to fly four Pakistani Catholics, whom he had never met, to Europe. When we make ourselves available for the Lord's use, He is faithful.

These events transpired in the weeks leading up to Thanksgiving 2019, a holiday that can provoke introspection, especially for those whose lives are marked with suffering and trials, for those who are uncertain about God's plans in their lives. Yet He is there, and He is not silent, as Protestant apologist Francis Schaeffer famously declared. The story of my Pakistani Catholic friends

[117] St. Alphonsus Liguori, *The Great Means of Salvation and of Perfection* in *Alphonsus Liguori: Selected Writings* (New York: Paulist Press, 1999), 299.

shows that He is there. If you ever wonder what God is doing, remember God's own words, spoken through the prophet Isaiah:

> Fear not, for I have redeemed you; I have called you by name, you are mine. When you pass through the waters, I will be with you; and through the rivers, they shall not overwhelm you; when you walk through fire you shall not be burned, and the flame shall not consume you. For I am the Lord your God, the Holy One of Israel, your Savior.... You are precious in my eyes, and honored, and I love you. (Isaiah 43:1–4)

In December 2019, only two weeks after their flight to Europe, Wilson sent me more remarkable news from the Netherlands: photos of school registration forms for his three children on their first day of school. He also sent me photos of his children's official Dutch school identification cards—proof that his family was legally in Europe. I remember the feelings of elation and freedom I experienced when I was given my driver's license after a few months of behind-the-wheel training and classroom instruction. I can only imagine the feeling of exhilaration Wilson's family must have felt. They were *free*. Free to worship, free to work, free to learn, free to walk the streets without fear of being rounded up and thrown into a Thai detention center or attacked by Pakistani Muslim extremists.

Wilson continued to send me holiday messages. On New Year's Eve 2019, he wrote to me: "Life is amazing. Love it. May the spirit of the season and the new year fill your heart with serenity and peace. Wish you a happy new year." I wish that I could have been with Wilson, to share his hope and excitement and his expectation that his family's long Lent was drawing to a close.

In February 2020, Wilson sent me photos of his children in art class, full of joy as they worked to paint models of owls. Later that month, he sent a video of a school costume party in the Netherlands, his children dressed up and smiling as they bounced and danced alongside their Dutch peers who were dressed as the Mario Brothers and various superheroes. One of his daughters playfully stuck her tongue out at the camera, a gesture of great significance: it is the kind of rebellious, silly thing children do only when they feel safe and secure. They also remained deeply pious: a later video, in April 2020, showed two of his children reciting the Divine Mercy Chaplet.

Since then, his family in Holland has waited for the Immigration and Naturalization Service, or IND, the Dutch immigration procedure. He told me that the refugee procedure in the Netherlands is "100% better" and that his family's lawyer there does not understand why their case was rejected by the UNHCR in Bangkok. Maryam and their three children live with Wilson's brother. Wilson praises the "good Catholic community" and says that parishioners there have been very good to his family. His children are already speaking Dutch with some proficiency. Though Maryam is not working, Wilson's brother serves as a traffic controller, a function similar to a traffic cop in the States.

Yet back in Bangkok, life is more difficult. Wilson's niece and nephew became ineligible to attend school in Bangkok when they turned sixteen in 2016. His mother's and sister Catherine's diabetes and his father's high blood pressure are continued concerns, as is his older sister Sarapheen's asthma. Wilson's parents—who are both in wheelchairs now—are free to go to the Netherlands but have been delayed because of the pandemic. Interpreters with both the UNHCR and other international organizations and embassies have continued to discriminate against Christians in favor of Muslims and Buddhists. Wilson also noted that some asylum-seeker families were attempting to resettle in Canada and Hungary—the former because of the success of Asia Bibi, the latter because of its pro-Christian government. I asked Wilson about his plan for his extended family in Thailand. He responded: "We don't know right now; we are just stuck here. God knows what His plan is for us."

Wilson noted two other pieces of news that signified new difficulties for the asylum-seeker community. The first was that the Kansan priest at Holy Redeemer who had been such a faithful advocate of the Catholic asylum seekers had passed away. The second was a surprising story about a Pakistani Christian asylum seeker who had been killed *in Thailand* in 2019 by Pakistani Muslim extremists. The Muslims—who traveled from Pakistan in search of this Christian—accused the man of blasphemy and murdered him in a remote Thai province. Wilson claimed the Thai authorities did nothing because the whole incident was an embarrassment to Thai immigration authorities.

The excitement and joy stemming from the resettlement of Wilson's immediate family was tempered by the continued uncertainty about the future of the rest of the family. Wilson himself could leave Bangkok at any time and join his family in Holland. But could he, in good conscience, leave his elderly parents and the rest of his extended family? On the other hand, would it be right for him to remain separated from his wife and children, potentially for years to come? These were hard questions.

But the question I kept asking myself was: When would we finally be able to say that Wilson's family had won? Would it be when all his family had been resettled in a country willing to take them? Or when all his family members had jobs with wages sufficient to support their family? Or once their children could attend schools and have a prospect at a better life? In my mind, I have a clear idea of what I consider the good life: freedom to worship God faithfully, professional and financial stability and security, opportunities for personal and vocational advancement. Yet, admittedly, billions of people across the globe, indeed the vast majority of people who have ever lived, have never attained the things I take for granted daily.

In the beginning of the Farewell Discourse in the Gospel of John, Jesus says to His disciples:

> In my Father's house are many rooms; if it were not so, would I have told you that I go to prepare a place for you? And when I go and prepare a place for you, I will come again and will take you to myself, that where I am you may be also. And you know the way where I am going. (John 14:2–4)

It would have been reasonable for Christ's disciples to suppose that He might be referring to a tangible, physical location. Perhaps He had determined to leave Judea and establish a new community, like the Essenes in the desert? Thomas seems to hint at this when he replies to Jesus: "Lord, we do not know where you are going; how can we know the way?"

But Jesus' reply suggests something radically different. He declares: "I am the way, and the truth, and the life; no one comes to the Father, but by me" (John 14:5–6). Fulfillment is not found by locating a new, perfect place. The good life is not a realization of worldly criteria, a nice home with a good job. Rather, Christ tells us, the good life is found in a person, Jesus Himself.

The genius of this divine destination helps us make sense of our world, which is filled with poverty, violence, and heartbreak. No matter our circumstances, no matter whether we live in suburban America, rural Pakistan, or urban Bangkok, Christ is there, present for us at all moments. He will never leave us or forsake us. His presence in our world is transformative not because of the potential to achieve a happy existence in this world, but because of His power to make sense of all things and to direct them to a transcendent, eternal end. He is the Alpha and the Omega.

I do want Wilson's family, all of them, to find the kind of happiness I view as normative as a middle-class American. Yet it is quite possible that such a dream will never be realized. And indeed, plenty of middle-class Americans experience shallow, broken lives, distant not only from God but from family, friends, and even themselves.

I know that Wilson, and Michael, if he ever finds a way, will have better, fuller lives living in the West. Yet Christ is just as present in the poverty of Bangkok and Karachi as He is in suburban Virginia, where I grew up and still live. Indeed, it was precisely because Christ was so vividly manifested in my Pakistani friends that I was drawn to them in the first place.

That is a truth powerful enough to engender hope in those who are tempted to lose it amid their painful trials. For that reason, I pray, alongside my Pakistani brethren, the Act of Hope:

O my God, relying on Your infinite goodness and promises, I hope to obtain pardon of my sins, the help of Your grace, and life everlasting, through the merits of Jesus Christ, my Lord and Redeemer.

10

Islamic Extremism Worldwide

This book has largely focused on the Muslim persecution of Christians in Pakistan, but this phenomenon is ubiquitous across the Muslim world. Brian Grim and Roger Finke, in their book *The Price of Freedom Denied: Religious Persecution and Conflict in the Twenty-First Century* (2010), demonstrate that a moderate to high level of violent religious persecution is found in 62 percent of Muslim-majority countries, compared with only 28 percent of Christian-majority countries.[118] Moreover, 78 percent of Muslim-majority countries have high levels of government restrictions on religious practices, compared with 43 percent of all other countries and 10 percent of Christian countries. According to Open Doors' 2018 World Watch List, each of the top ten countries with the worst records of religious persecution of Christians is predominantly Muslim, with the exception of North Korea, and most are in the Middle East and Africa. The only parts of the Muslim world where there is significant freedom for Christians are West Africa and Indonesia, though there has been increased violence even in those places in recent years against Christian

[118] Many of the details in this section can be found in Chalk, "Muslim-Led Persecution."

communities. In many Muslim countries, conversion to Christianity is a capital crime, according to a law that directly stems from widely held interpretations of the Quran.

Such persecution is visible, even in Muslim-majority democracies often lauded for their supposed pluralism, openness, and tolerance. Take a recent example from Indonesia, a country I twice visited while we lived in Thailand. Indonesia is a massive archipelago of 17,508 islands, and Muslims make up about 87 percent of the population of 268 million. Christians make up about 10 percent of the population. In 2016, the governor of Indonesia's capital, Jakarta, Basuki Tjahaja Purnama, better known by his nickname "Ahok," declared his intention to campaign again for the gubernatorial position. Many pundits considered Ahok a possible future candidate for Indonesian president, as his gubernatorial predecessor, Joko Widodo, or "Jokowi," had also been governor of Jakarta.

On September 27, 2016, Ahok publicly claimed that some citizens would not vote for him because they were being "threatened and deceived" by those using a Quranic verse and variations of it. Ahok exhorted voters not to be manipulated by religious leaders who were exploiting the verse to justify a widely publicized assertion that Muslims should not allow non-Muslim political leaders. The video, uploaded to a provincial governorate YouTube page, was later edited by university lecturer Buni Yani. The lecturer omitted several of Ahok's words from that video, and the edited version gave the impression that Ahok had suggested the Quranic verse itself was misleading, rather than the Islamic leaders who were citing it.

The video went viral, and a subsequent poll reported that almost half of Indonesian citizens labeled it an insult to the Quran. Many threatened to lynch Ahok. In October 2016, Ahok publicly apologized for his comments, but it was too late. The Jakarta governor was formally charged with blasphemy, and his trial began in December 2016. Ahok's comments, his detractors argued, were a violation of Indonesia's 1965 blasphemy law. On May 9, 2017, the North Jakarta District Court found Ahok guilty of blasphemy and "inciting violence" and sentenced him to two years in prison. A later appeal was rejected, and Ahok was unable to finish his term as Jakarta's governor. Despite international outcries by human rights organizations, Ahok was not released until January 24, 2019.[119]

Why is Christianity so challenging for many Muslims? Religion scholar David Pinault points to part of the answer in his book *The Crucifix on Mecca's Front Porch: A Christian's Companion for the Study of Islam*.[120] Pinault discusses a set of traits visible in the origins of Islam and the Quran that play a prominent role in its contemporary manifestations: rage, revenge, and violence. He notes that Muhammad and his message initially encountered much resistance and ridicule in Mecca. He found a more welcome hearing in Medina, where he soon gathered a following that enabled him to take revenge against his Meccan enemies. Muhammad upended ancient Jahiliya custom among Arabs that had promoted the ransoming, rather than the killing, of prisoners

---

[119] Kate Lamb, "Ahok, Jakarta's Former Governor, Released After Jail Term for Blasphemy," *Guardian* (U.S.), January 23, 2019, https://www.theguardian.com/world/2019/jan/24/ahok-jakartas-former-governor-released-after-jail-term-for-blasphemy.

[120] David Pinault, *The Crucifix on Mecca's Front Porch: A Christian's Companion for the Study of Islam* (San Francisco: Ignatius Press, 2018). Many of the details in this section can be found in Casey Chalk, "Shame and Redemption," *Touchstone* (May/June 2019).

of war. His thoughts on this are reflected in a Quranic verse: "It is not appropriate for a prophet to take prisoners of war until he has made a great slaughter in the land" (8:67). He began a campaign of revenge aimed at those who had either mocked him or promoted pagan customs, what the Quran calls "frivolous stories." He then ordered the brutal murder of his enemies across Arabia. Pinault notes in these stories Muhammad's "lingering resentment and rage" toward those who had dishonored him. Other scholars have seen the same thing. For example, W. M. Watt, a scholar sympathetic to Muhammad, observes that he was "specially sensitive to intellectual or literary attacks."[121]

This is profoundly important, says Pinault, because Muslims have always viewed the details of Muhammad's life as "paradigmatic in Islam ... provid[ing] examples for the pious to follow in structuring their own lives as faithful believers." Indeed, both Sunni and Shia Muslims view Muhammad as a "moral exemplar whose behavior is to be imitated." Ergo, if Muhammad is exceptionally concerned with attacks on his honor and that of the Quranic message, and if he models that an appropriate response to such challenges is revenge and violence, it is not surprising that we experience the same from his followers.

Furthermore, there is no greater shame or dishonor, in the Muslim mind, than the belief that God would condescend to become human and be crucified on a cross. As Pinault notes, to make such a claim is equivalent to "claiming a prophet is *majnun*," that is, possessed by a jinni, or malevolent spirit. Indeed, Muhammad had several of his opponents crucified as particularly emphatic demonstrations of retribution.

[121] W. M. Watt, *Muhammad: Prophet and Stateman* (Oxford, UK: Oxford University Press, 1961), 123.

Interestingly, Muhammad felt a deep sense of kinship with many prophets of the Bible as well as with Jesus Himself. But he believed that all prophets are vindicated, so an ignoble death —like that experienced by Christ—was a stumbling block for him. In fact, in the Quran, the portrayal of Jesus is reminiscent of the Docetist heresy: Jesus is not actually crucified; He simply appears to be. He is never dishonorably killed on a cross but is, in fact, victorious over His enemies.

Indeed, the very Cross of Christ, which Christians celebrate, is a shameful symbol for Muslims. Not only is it derided in the Quran, but throughout Islamic history it is consistently regarded with scorn. One Muslim traveler visiting the Crusader stronghold of Acre described the city as swarming with impure pigs (an unclean animal for Muslims) and crosses. Raised aloft by Crusader armies, and imprinted on their military regalia, the cross also became a "symbol of a hated foe." Indeed, Muslim soldiers during the Crusades routinely scorned and desecrated crosses, often in the sight of their enemies. When the famous Muslim leader Saladin conquered Jerusalem in 1187, he had the cross on the summit of the Temple of the Lord cast down, carried around the city, and beaten with sticks for two days. To this day, Pinault notes, much Muslim apologetic literature ridicules the cross, while Islamic extremists such as ISIS crucify their enemies.

Of course, Muslim countries are not the only places where Christians are persecuted. As John L. Allen Jr. observes in his superb book *The Global War on Christians: Dispatches from the Front Lines of Anti-Christian Persecution*, Christians suffer in many non-Muslim-majority countries as well.[122] China and North Korea, for example, are both oppressive totalitarian states, and both

---

[122] Allen, *Global War*, 202.

brutally repress Christianity. "Instead of Islam being the lone protagonist, the global war on Christians is fueled by a complex galaxy of heterogeneous forces, each of which has its own reasons for seeing Christians as a threat," Allen notes.

Yet, as Michel Houellebecq's frightening but brilliant 2015 novel *Submission* reminds us, the very word *Islam* means "submission," and that is exactly what many who practice it seek to achieve: unconditional submission. Aggressive, intolerant forms of Islam are practiced across the Muslim world, which is why Christians are now fleeing countries such as Egypt, Iraq, Pakistan, and Syria by the thousands.

Islam as a religiopolitical force once threatened the gates of Europe at Vienna. A new extremist strain has emerged that is a global threat to Christianity worldwide.

Conclusion

*The mystery of the Church is not a truth to be confined
to the realms of speculative theology. It must be lived, so
that the faithful may have a kind of intuitive experience
of it, even before they come to understand it clearly.*

—St. Paul VI, *Ecclesiam Suam* 37

Why did I write this book? Primarily, it was because I believe
the Holy Spirit called me to share the story of the persecuted
Church in Pakistan and its connection to Bangkok's asylum-
seeker crisis—and perhaps He called you to learn about it too.
But I also wrote it because I hold a graduate degree in theology,
a discipline that can sometimes seem esoteric and impractical.
By applying my theological training to my experiences working with Pakistani Christian asylum seekers, I wanted to share
my love of theology, which, in the end, is a love of the things
of God.

Before I end the book, then, I offer a few final thoughts on the
situation of asylum seekers and refugees in Bangkok as of summer
2021 and a few reflections on ecumenism, Islam, and personal
spirituality. I also offer a few suggestions for those interested in
contributing to efforts to support the global persecuted Church.

The Persecuted

My friend Fr. John Murray, an Augustinian priest and migrant advocate, is probably best equipped to speak to the current status of the migrant crisis in Thailand. Below is an excerpt from a document he maintains and shares with those looking for an explanation of the crisis as it stands.

The managing of the urban refugee situation is presently under a state of flux as the Thai government has approved what is called the National Screening Mechanism which is about the government accepting the role of screening and registering refugees. This will be a local process run with UNHCR support and according to international standards. While this has occurred due to lobbying by Thai NGOs with UNHCR and seen as a positive step forward, nobody knows exactly what this means for the refugees and asylum seekers themselves. This mechanism will be implemented mid-2020 but under a cloud of confusion and lack of clarity.

This population is both asylum seeker and refugee. At the end of December 2019, UNHCR named that there were 4,200 urban refugees and 800 urban asylum seekers here in Bangkok. Amongst the refugees, the populations significantly represented were Pakistani, Vietnamese, Palestinian and Somali. Amongst the asylum seeker population, they came mostly from Vietnam, Cambodia, China and Pakistan. This shows the diversity of the population. While the population is small in number, it experiences an incredibly high level of need. Its basic challenge remains that of daily survival—paying the rent, buying the food.

While here, the population is under the UN process of determination of refugee status followed by possible resettlement which is less and less likely in the present world context. UNHCR now no longer talks of any promise of resettlement. Rather its emphasis now is that of long term protection for refugees staying in Thailand under their protection.

UNHCR is experiencing a consistent decrease in its available budget. This results in its continually cutting back its services and assessing what it can provide into the future. Bottom line is that less and less assistance is being offered by UNHCR locally due to its own resources being stretched to the limit within the global refugee context and under the pressures of the world politick.

As the pandemic has progressed over the past 12 months, we see how it impacts more so upon the most vulnerable in our world, including the urban refugee population in Bangkok. This has been seen in their losing any scarce employment they may have had with its loss of income. So their situation becomes even more dire, which has led to even more worrying concerns in their accompanying further loss of dignity, and some even considering suicide. Tragic. Still not all bad news as some are positively pursuing progress in their quest for a new home somewhere safe. I continue to pray and believe.

Moreover, Fr. John tells me that the UNHCR is working on an even tighter budget than it was when I was there, between 2014 and 2017. This means there are even fewer resources and staff capable of helping families like those of Wilson and Michael.

This book has highlighted their stories because I am intimately familiar with their lives. But it is most important to remember that there are thousands of other Pakistani Catholic families, just like Wilson's and Michael's, currently living illegally in Bangkok. Many of their stories are just as harrowing. Their faith is equally pious. Their needs are equally immediate. Even if Wilson, Michael, and their families secure a better life, there is still much work to be done. What is happening to Christians in Bangkok and Pakistan and many other places is indeed a humanitarian *crisis*, and international headlines regularly attest to it.

☙

On May 22, 2020, Pakistani citizen Sohail Latif, a pastor as well as the founder and chairman of River of Life Christian Church (Anglican), was imprisoned without charges. He was reportedly seized by Pakistani authorities who burst into his house in the middle of the night while he, his wife, and their five children were asleep.[123] Latif, whose hearing was postponed in late August after a police officer did not appear at his trial, contracted an illness, possibly coronavirus, while in Pakistani prison, according to a report by Christian news website Juicy Ecumenism.[124]

Only a few weeks later, on September 8, a sessions court in Lahore sentenced Asif Pervaiz, a thirty-seven-year-old Christian man, to death after convicting him of sending text messages containing "blasphemous content." Pervaiz had been in custody since 2013 because of blasphemy charges leveled against him by the supervisor of the garment factory where he was once employed.

---

[123] Faith McDonnell, "Save Pakistani Pastor Sohail, Imprisoned without Charges Since May 22," *Stream*, August 19, 2020, https://stream.org/save-pastor-sohail/.

[124] Faith McDonnell, "Save Pakistani Pastor Sohail, Imprisoned without Charges Since May 22," Juicy Ecumenism, August 21, 2020, https://juicyecumenism.com/2020/08/21/save-pakistani-pastor-sohail-imprisoned-without-charges-since-may-22/.

The supervisor accused Pervaiz of sending text messages with derogatory content about the Prophet Muhammad. The court order declared that Pervaiz would serve a further three-year prison term for "misusing" his phone to send the derogatory text message, as well as pay a fine of fifty thousand Pakistani rupees, or about three hundred U.S. dollars. Then, the court ordered, "he shall be hanged by his neck till his death."

Pervaiz denied the allegations, claiming that his supervisor, Muhammad Saeed Khokher, had pressured him to convert to Islam, overtures Pervaiz says he refused. He then quit working at the factory but was confronted by Khokher with continued exhortations to convert. After Pervaiz's further refusals, Khokher accused him of sending the blasphemous text messages. Khokher, for his part, denied that he pressured Pervaiz to convert and said that none of the other Christian employees working at the factory had made similar allegations.[125]

The stories of Sohail Latif and Asif Pervaiz share much in common with Asia Bibi, Wilson William, and Michael D'Souza. All these Christians describe Muslim bullying and coercion. All of them suffered allegations of blasphemy against Islam or Muhammad—charges that seem a little far-fetched, given that Christians face *execution* if found guilty of such an offense. All of them encountered negligence, persecution, or both, from Pakistani government authorities who were sometimes complicit in the anti-Christian activities of extremist Muslims.

Sadly, what this means is that even if Bangkok's Pakistani Christian refugee crisis were to be solved, widespread discrimination and

---

[125] AFP, "Lahore Court Sentences Christian Man to Death over Blasphemous Texts," *Dawn*, September 8, 2020, https://www. dawn.com/news/1578596.

persecution against followers of Christ are likely to continue in Pakistan. Many of these Christians, under both social and political pressure, will continue to flee their homes, desperate to find a haven where they can escape oppression and build a new life.

⁂

Since returning to the United States,[126] I've often remembered with fondness the ecumenical efforts to address the humanitarian crisis in Bangkok. The plight of the oppressed in Thailand served as a common call to care for the Body of Christ. It drew people from varied religious, national, and linguistic backgrounds and united them to the same people and places. Catholics, Evangelicals, and Mormons were all on the D'Souzas' visitor list at the IDC, and never once during all those visits did anyone think to debate or condemn another religious tradition. We were simply too busy doing God's work.

This is not to say that debate and criticism are not healthy, essential aspects of ecumenism. Indeed, I continue to engage in such efforts, especially through my writing. But just as we must band together to combat our current sociocultural crisis in the West, where the secular, progressivist, anti-God enemy wages full-scale war on Christ and His Church, we must consider our differences carefully wherever the work of Christ is concerned. Such has been the clarion call of Christian ecumenical movements since the First Crusade, Lepanto, and the Second World War motivated disparate forces. Alexios I Komnenos, Pope Pius V, and Dietrich Bonhoeffer all were able to perceive the dangers that threatened the very survival of the Body of Christ. I witnessed

---

[126] Many of the details in this section can be found in Chalk, "Jesus in Thailand."

that same broad-minded perception in so many of the Christian men and women I worked with in Bangkok.

On the other hand, this ecumenical experience, aimed at addressing the needs of the persecuted and the marginalized, also helped me understand the biblical mandate to care for those in the direst need. Scripture is filled with stories of immigrant peoples looking for deliverance: Abraham migrated to Egypt during a great famine (Gen. 12:10); the entire Israelite community, numbering seventy people, later fled once again to Egypt in the face of another famine (Gen. 42–47); and David, on the run from King Saul, sought asylum with the king of Gath (1 Sam. 21:10). Most importantly for salvation history, the Holy Family fled the murderous King Herod by seeking refuge in Egypt (Matt. 2:13–23).

Of course, worldly politics are always complicated. All pro-immigration policies, especially those that threaten the physical or economic security of a nation, are not inherently divinely sanctioned; nor are anti-immigration policies that seek to secure borders or protect domestic workforces censured by the biblical record.[127] Nevertheless, the desire to help asylum seekers and refugees, which was evident in every Christian tradition I encountered in Thailand, suggests to me that God aims to place

---

[127] For an overview of Catholic social teaching on immigration, see Fr. Thomas Betz, O.F.C., "Catholic Social Teaching on Immigration and the Movement of Peoples," United States Conference of Catholic Bishops, http://www.usccb.org/issues-and-action/human-life-and-dignity/immigration/catholic-teaching-on-immigration-and-the-movement-of-peoples.cfm. For a thoughtful, well-researched analysis on the perils of large-scale immigration to societies seeking to preserve a unique political, social, economic, or religious identity, see Lawrence M. Mead, *Burdens of Freedom: Cultural Difference and American Power* (New York: Encounter Books, 2019).

in any soul touched by His Holy Spirit a passion for the lost, the oppressed, and the wayfaring.

Furthermore, the current Western immigration policies, as they pertain to those suffering religious persecution, seem to me ill-considered. If Germany can absorb hundreds of thousands of Muslim refugees, why cannot Germany, or other countries, including the United States, accept a few thousand persecuted Christian minorities who are waiting, and hoping, in Bangkok? Indeed, given their small numbers and shared cultural heritage with the Christian West, they would appear to be ripe candidates for an eager politician looking to bolster his compassion credentials.

Thankfully, there has been some welcome news since we departed Bangkok. The Canada-based *Catholic Register* reported in September 2019 that "at least eight dioceses have pledged to raise money and gather volunteers to give a new Canadian home to up to 65 families eligible for resettlement" for Pakistani Christians in Bangkok. The pledge of support came "in response to a mission trip by the Office for Refugees, Archdiocese of Toronto to Bangkok to vet candidates for resettlement," which then triggered a *Catholic Register* series about Christian asylum seekers in Thailand who had fled Pakistan's harsh blasphemy laws. "When their suffering is brought to [Canadian Catholics'] attention, as was done through *The Catholic Register*, people want to respond," said Office for Refugees, Archdiocese of Toronto director Deacon Rudy Ovcjak. He added: "You can't help but be moved by the suffering of this community — to know not only their suffering in Pakistan but their ongoing suffering in Bangkok."[128]

---

[128] Michael Swan, "Canadians Respond to Refugees' Plight," *Catholic Register*, September 25, 2019, https://www.catholicregister.org/item/30327-canadians-respond-to-refugees-plight.

I pray that the United States, and the Church in America, will take notice of that act of compassion by our northern neighbors. A strong, coordinated effort to provide material support to this vulnerable community would be a welcome recognition that they are indeed our brothers and sisters in Christ and that we remember them. Separated by great distances, we can often feel helpless in the midst of anti-Christian violence that has soaked the ground from Lahore to Libya with martyrs' blood. But through our support, and our prayers, we can make sure their voices, and the voices of their kin in Bangkok, ring louder than any terrorist threats.

⁓

Since returning to the safety and comfort of the United States, to this blessed and prosperous land, my family has continued to seek out opportunities to serve those brothers and sisters in Christ who suffer in silence. Yet our inspiration will always be people like Michael, Rosemary, Rochelle, Miles, and Reine; Wilson, Maryam, Stephanie, Angel, and Arun; William Masih and and Gulzar Bibi, Sarapheen, Catherine, Sania, Sunil, Sameer, and Bulbul; Sonam, Urshia, and Urshaman; and Naomi. They changed our lives.

For it is in their faces that we saw the face of the risen Lord.

Postscript

Where Do We Go from Here?

There are several practical ways that readers can help perse-cuted Christians like Michael, Wilson, and the many others I met during my years in Thailand. The first is prayer. Prayer has valuable effects for both the one who prays and the one for whom the prayers are offered. As the *Catechism of the Catholic Church* explains:

> In the New Covenant, prayer is the living relationship of the children of God with their Father who is good beyond measure, with his Son Jesus Christ and with the Holy Spirit. The grace of the Kingdom is "the union of the entire holy and royal Trinity ... with the whole human spirit." Thus, the life of prayer is the habit of being in the presence of the thrice-holy God and in communion with him.[129]

In our communion with God in prayer, we ourselves are trans-formed by placing ourselves in His presence. By uniting ourselves to Christ in prayer, we unite ourselves to His Mystical Body — and to the body of the persecuted Church.

---

[129] *Catechism of the Catholic Church*, no. 2565, quoting St. Gregory of Nazianzus, *Oratio*, 16, 9: PG 35, 945.

The Persecuted

There is an old Catholic aphorism: *Lex orandi, lex credendi* (the law of prayer is the law of belief). One meaning of this is that as we intentionally pray for our Christian brothers and sisters in need, especially if it is done not only individually but corporately and liturgically, our Christian communities will be changed to become more aware and attuned to the persecuted. Such prayers, argues John L. Allen Jr., "help raise consciousness and steel resolve."[130]

We also must not underestimate the power of prayer to effect change for those for whom we intercede. The story of Wilson and his family is instructive. Wilson's family prayed and fasted for years so that God might save them from their plight. The Lord heard their prayers, and now Wilson's wife and three children are living safely in the Netherlands.

We must continue to ask God for His grace and mercy, including that one day all the members of Wilson's and Michael's families will be given a new home. I am convinced, more than ever, that such prayers are not offered in vain. Indeed, Jesus tells His apostles on the night of His betrayal: "Whatever you ask in my name, I will do it, that the Father may be glorified in the Son; if you ask anything in my name, I will do it" (John 14:13–4).

We should also demand more from the media, both secular and religious. Allen observes:

> The scope and scale of the global war on Christians is almost invariably news to audiences in the West.... Most people are staggered to hear that a leading estimate says that eleven Christians are killed somewhere in the world every hour, or that 80 percent of all acts of religious persecution in the world today are directed at Christians.[131]

---

[130] Allen, *Global War*, 282.
[131] Allen, *Global War*, 279.

I likewise noted this disparity in news coverage on the plight of persecuted Christian minorities in one of my articles on Michael for the *Federalist* in 2018.[132]

But we need not wait for others. We can post stories about persecution of Christians on our personal social media. We can subscribe to publications that report on Christian persecution in order to support their work and stay abreast of the latest developments, and we can distribute those publications to our local churches, Bible studies, and libraries. We can write letters to the editor expressing our interest in more reporting on the global war on Christians. We could propose writing articles on the persecution of Christians for our parish bulletin, diocesan newspaper, or for a blog or website. When we see publications reporting these kinds of stories, we should commend and publicize them wherever we can.

We can also continue to advocate on behalf of persecuted Christians.[133] As I have argued in the *American Conservative*, we remain a nation with one of the most vocal Christian political communities in the West: one-third of America's citizens still consider her to be a Christian nation.[134] To be faithful to that identity, we should voice our concern about policy decisions that might disproportionately harm Christians in other countries, especially where they are already vulnerable minorities. Allen argues: "Christians can insist that the defense of religious freedom

---

[132] Chalk, "Muslim-Led Persecution."

[133] Allen, *Global War*, 289.

[134] Casey Chalk, "How Much More Christian Blood Must Our Interventions Spill?," *American Conservative*, September 25, 2019, https://www.theamericanconservative.com/articles/how-much-more-christian-blood-must-our-interventions-spill/.

internationally become a more central element of the foreign policy of Western governments."[135]

We can also urge our political representatives to pursue policies that protect persecuted Christians and other threatened religious minorities. Allen again suggests demanding policies on refugee admission and resettlement that "recognize persecuted Christians as a protected category."[136] Our experience with the U.S. House Foreign Affairs Subcommittee on Africa, Global Health, Global Human Rights, and International Organizations hearing, in which Michael's case was presented by the Jubilee Campaign, demonstrated how woefully ignorant many of our representatives are about the fact that Christians are the most persecuted religious group on the planet.

Finally, I should also mention in closing that the financial needs of the persecuted global Church are immense. There are many charitable organizations to which interested Christians can donate their money and witness an immediate impact on the welfare of the faithful around the world. These include the Aid to the Church in Need (www.churchinneed.org), Catholic Near East Welfare Association (CNEWA; www.cnewa.org), the Knights of Columbus (ChristiansatRisk.org), and Barnabas Fund (https://barnabasfund.org/).[137]

---

[135] Allen, *Global War*, 289.
[136] Allen, *Global War*, 291.
[137] Further information on these organizations can be found on the United States Conference of Catholic Bishops website: http://www.usccb.org/issues-and-action/human-life-and-dignity/global-issues/middle-east/christians-in-the-middle-east/upload/AidOrganizations.pdf.

Acknowledgments

I would not have been able to write this story without the trust, charity, and friendship extended to me by the Pakistani asylum-seeker and refugee community in Bangkok. I am especially grateful to the families of Wilson William and Michael D'Souza, who so graciously allowed my wife and me to enter into their lives and provide, imperfectly, our love and support to them through their many trials. They are my heroes. Thank you also to all those Pakistani Christians whose stories have yet to be told, who suffer in silence for our Lord Jesus.

Thank you to all the editors and journalists who have been willing to feature stories on the plight of persecuted Pakistani Christians: Pieter Vree (*New Oxford Review*), David Mills (*Ethika Politika*), Mattias Caro (*Ethika Politika*), Robert Royal (the *Catholic Thing*), Joy Pullman (the *Federalist*), James Kushiner (*Touchstone*), Michael Warren Davis (*Crisis Magazine*), and Kathleen Hattrup (*Aleteia*), among others. Thank you also to *New Oxford Review*, *Crisis Magazine*, the *American Conservative*, and the *Federalist*, which have invited me to join their editorial mission and have given me so many opportunities to feature and improve my writing over the years.

The Persecuted

Thank you to my many spiritual mentors and inspirations who advised and helped me throughout this process: Fr. Thomas Joseph White, O.P., who brought me back to the Catholic Church of my youth; Fr. Ramon Baez, my spiritual director for almost a decade; Fr. John Murray, O.S.A., an Aussie priest who serves the migrant community of Bangkok; and Fr. Frank Bird, a Marist, Kiwi priest serving Burmese migrant workers on the Thai-Burma border.

Thank you to those mentors from my Protestant days who did so much to inspire in me a love for Christ and His Gospel: Kelly Scott, Dr. David Coffin, Paul Wolfe, Dr. Howard Griffith (RIP), and Dr. Stephen Nichols. I must also express gratitude to the faculty at the Notre Dame Graduate School of Theology at Christendom College, including Dr. Robert J. Matava, Fr. Sebastian Carnazzo, Dr. James Arias, Dr. Donald Prudlo, and Dr. Kristin Burns (RIP).

Thank you to my close friends who listened to my stories about Bangkok and Pakistan and encouraged me as I wrote: Barrett and Beth Turner, Zachary Kuenzli, Jim and Sam Van Dyke, Steve Petullo, Michael Horvath, Nicholas Lee, Adam Zerbinopoulos, Matt Brock, Brian Torro, Emile Doak, and Robert Singler.

Thank you, too, to Dr. Paul Thigpen, whose guidance, wisdom, and editing skills, gained from having written more than fifty published books, were integral to my writing this story. Thank you to Dr. David Pinault for his valuable expertise on Islam and his suggestions for this book. Thank you to Pierro Tozzi and Ann Buwalda for their professional legal assistance on behalf of Pakistani Christians. Thank you to Drew Oliver, Michael Warren Davis, and Nora Malone for their excellent editorial assistance in preparing this book for publication, and to all the fantastic folks at Sophia Institute Press who labored on my behalf.

Acknowledgments

To my in-laws, Stephen and Christine Caveness, who made Claire's and my concern for persecuted Pakistani Catholics their own and gave selflessly of their time, energy, and money to help Wilson's and Michael's families.

Thank you to the many family members who prayed for me, mentored me, and encouraged me as a student, a Christian, a husband, and a father: my grandparents, Jack and Reta Fitzpatrick and Joseph and Irene Chalk; Hartley and Lorraine Dewey; Jody Chalk; Stephanie Chalk; Kevin Fitzpatrick; Derek McCall; Tara McCall; and Bill and Barbara Hosack.

I am particularly grateful to my mother, Christine, and my father, Daniel, who, while I was in high school, exposed me to the plight of persecuted Christians around the world. I dedicate this book also to the memory of my late father, who, whenever he was presented with details of the suffering of the global church, always sought eagerly to give and pray for the relief of the persecuted.

Thank you to my wife, Claire. She was patient beyond measure in helping me to devote the countless hours required to complete this book. This story is hers as well because she gave so much of herself and her love, both to me and to our Pakistani friends. This story would not be possible to tell without everything she has done and continues to do.

Thank you also to my children, Annemarie, Thomas, Elizabeth, and Lawrence, who so often sought their father's attention and were so often rebuffed as I worked hard to complete this project. I promise to make it up to them!

And thank you to Jesus. You are my Lord and Savior, as You are for so many Pakistani Christians. In all my sins and doubts, You have remained faithful to me in Your steadfast love. I pray that You will see us all through to the end.

Appendix A

Data Substantiating the Persecution of Wilson William's Family

The following pages include documents that substantiate the story of Wilson William and his family as well as photos of the families of Wilson and of Casey Chalk.

Excerpt from Urdu-language Pakistan newspaper Janbaz: "In the area of Pahar Ganj, a Pakistani organization and the Christian community had tension due to a Christian man named Younas Masih who disrespected the holy Quran and tore the papers of the book."

Fatwa issued by Mufti Haji Sheikh Amin Ahmed, at the Jamia Masjid al Muqadas Mosque. It reads that the Mufti "has issued this as a death penalty against Nasreen Maryam and against her family members named William Masih, Wilson William, Gulzar William, Catherine Salamat, and Sania Salamat for disrespecting the holy Quran, tearing and burning the holy papers from the Quran. Therefore this whole family has done a sin against Islam, so this family is eligible to die, and anyone who finds this pagan family and kills them will go directly to heaven."

The Persecuted

Excerpt from the Urdu-language Pakistan newspaper Qumirala: *"Sania Salamat, while on her way to church, was approached by a mullah who tried to kidnap her and rape her but due to the crowd he was not able to do so."*

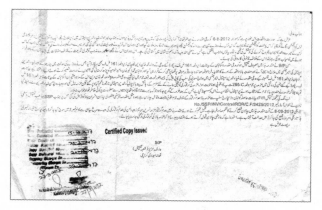

On this and the following pages are court documents regarding the alleged blasphemy by Wilson's wife, Maryam.

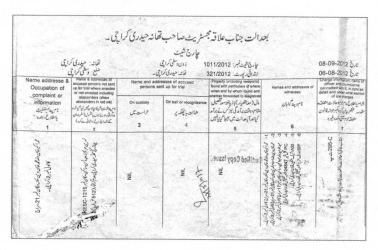

IN THE COURT OF ~~VIIK~~ CIVIL JUDGE & JUDICIAL
MAGISTRATE, CENTRAL, KARACHI.

Cr. Case No. Nil / 2012

Muhammad Akbar Khan...................................Complainant

VERSUS

Nasreen Maryam..Accused

FIR No.321/2012
U/S   295-C, PPC
PS   Haidery

Certified Copy Issued

Certified Copy Issued

ORDER
12.09.2012

Case Called, Muhammad Akbar Khan complainant, ADPP and Investigation Officer are present, I. O submitted Interim Challan against accused, namely, Miss Nasreen Maryam, her name was in the column No.2 of challan with red ink, as absconder Under Section 512 Cr.P.C., I.O. submitted that he went to the Ziauddin Hospital where the accused lady is working as female nurse, as well as twice time attempted her residence, which remains closed, he inquired from neighbors about her whereabouts but no one knows. Heard complainant, who supported his contention already disclosed in FIR. I.O is directed to make efforts for the arrest of accused, Miss Nasreen Maryam. Matter is adjourned to 28.09.2012.

Sd. /
Civil Judge & Judicial Magistrate
_____, Central, Karachi.

Certified Copy, issued

VI Civil Judge & Judicial Magistrate
Karachi (Cantt)
27/3/2017

ORDER
28.09.2012

Case Called ADPP and Investigation Officer are present, I.O. requested for grant of time for compliance of court order dated 12.09.2012, four weeks time allowed to the I.O, with direction to make possible measures and assure arrest of accused Miss Nasreen Maryam till next date. Matter put up to 30.10.2012.

Sd. /___
Civil Judge & Judicial Magistrate
VII /₁₂⁻, Central, Karachi.

Certified Copy Issued

Order
30.10.2012

Case called ADPP and Investigation Officer are present, heard both, I.O. submitted report that he approached to the admin of Ziauddin Hospital, North Nazimabad, Karachi for arrest of accused Nasreen Maryam, whereat he was informed that Miss Nasreen Maryam Female Nurse on 02.10.2012 resigned her services with the Hospital. Thereafter I.O. approached to the residence of accused wherefrom he collected information from two neighbors, whose statements are provided with copies of CNIC, they informed that Miss Nasreen Maryam and her whole family about a month ago shifted their residence to another place, but they were not aware regarding her new address. I.O. made efforts for her arrest but could not succeed, hence the accused, Miss Nasreen Maryam W/O Wilson Masih declared as proclaimed offender under section 87 and 88 Cr.P.C, such notice be affixed to the notice board of the court. Come up on 29.11.2012.

Sd. /___
Civil Judge & Judicial Magistrate
VIII   , Central, Karachi.

Certified Copy Issued

<u>Order</u>
<u>29.11.2012</u>

Case called ADPP and Investigation Officer are present, compliance
under Section 87 and 88 Cr.P.C were made, after hectic efforts I.O
failed to arrest the accused, Miss Nasreen Maryam wife of Wilson
Masih, according to the I.O there is no chance of the arrest of the
accused in near future, hence the R&P be kept to the dormant file.

Sd. /___
Civil Judge & Judicial Magistrate
, Central, Karachi

Certified Copy Issued

> ## ST. JUDE'S CHURCH,
> ## BLOCK-P NORTH NAZIMABAD,
> ## KARACHI-74700
> PHONE: ~~6631693~~ 0301-287452
>
> PAKISTAN...24./.12./...2002...........
>
> ### TO WHOM IT MAY CONCERN
>
> In Karachi and the whole of Pakistan religious intolerance is growing day by day. As a consequence my Parishioner, NASRIN w/o WILSON has been living in fear because of an accusation made against her under the BLASPHEMY LAW. For four months they have tried to hide themselves (the family). Now they were forced to make the descision of leaving Pakistan to go elsewhere.
>
> Their case is genuine and any assistance provided them will help them in their difficult circumstances.
>
> (Fr) R. D'Souza
> PARISH PRIEST

Letter from Karachi-based parish priest Fr. D'Souza regarding blasphemy allegations of Wilson's family and their subsequent persecution

The Persecuted

Plot # 2/57, Raymond Street,
Opp. Cambridge Mall, Saddar, Karachi-74400.
E-mail: ncjppakistankarachi@hotmail.com

NATIONAL COMMISSION FOR JUSTICE AND PEACE

Date: December 21, 2012

TO WHOM IT MAY CONCERN

This is to certify that Mr. Wilson s/o William resident of house # 1215, Block Q, Pahargunj Karachi since last 30 years.

As he told us that he has faced difficult situation at his house since March 2011, when two heavily bearded and tall men wearing the caps use for pray entered his house with guns and they opened a torn Quran and thrust into his brother Mr. Younas s/o William's hands, and they quickly hold Younas and said, we will take you with us, fortunately he was able to run and jump in another house to secure himself the persons left from his house immediately and threatened that he will face the consequences and he will come again and take him with us.

Because of this incident Mr. Younas left his homeland in May 2011, and after that the whole family got fraternal and had to leave their house at night only, now they are threaten Mr. Wilson s/o William to call back his brother otherwise we will kill you and your whole family.

As per his Parish Priest they are not more able to stay here, otherwise it will not good for his family.

They need protection and assistance, please assists them in any regards.

It will be highly appreciated.

Noel Allance
Diocesan Coordinator

National Commission for Justice and Peace
Plot No. 2/57, Raymond Street,
Opp. Cambridge Mall, Saddar, Karachi-74400.
E-mail: ncjppakistankarachi@hotmail.com

Letter written by the Pakistan-based National Commission for Justice and Peace regarding the persecution suffered by Wilson's family, including his brother Younas

วัดพระมหาไถ่
HOLY REDEEMER CHURCH
123/15 ซอยร่วมฤดี 5 ถ.วิทยุ เขตปทุมวัน กรุงเทพฯ 10330 : 123/15 Soi Ruamrudi 5, Wittayu rd., Pathumwan, Bangkok 10330 THAILAND
Tel : 02-651-5251-3 Fax : 02-651-5255 Email : redeemerbangkok@hotmail.com http://www.holyredeemerbangkok.net

10 May 2014

The UNHCR

Bangkok Thailand

To whom it may concern,

        One and half year ago the poor family of Mr Masih William come to Holy redeemer church Bangkok .I know these people because they are regular membesr of our church. They proved themselves as true catholic.

Their priest, the Pakistani fr.Dsauza write in his letter that their case is genuine. Their two nieces of the same family name, sonam and urisha, are burnt in her house. These also are victim of the same tragic persecution.

In March 2014, Bishop Joseph from Karachi Pakistan, visited our church and explained the situation to us espically about this family. He verifies that all documents are genuine. These poor people came to Bangkok to seek humanitarian helps.

So, please help them and provide them protection and consider their case with kind heart.

Sincerely yours

Phaiboon

Father Augustine phaiboon C.S.S.R.Ph.D.

(Pastor of Holy Redeemer church Bangkok ,Thailand)

A letter written by Fr. Phaiboon, pastor of Holy Redeemer Catholic Church in Bangkok, to the UNHCR regarding the plight of Wilson and his family

Catholic Archdiocese of Karachi

July 20, 2017

To, Mr. Peter Trotter
Senior Protection Officer
UNHCR Office,
Thailand.

Subject: **REQUEST TO RE-OPEN THE FILE OF MR. WILSON**
LEGAL/RSD /14/0048, UNHCH

Registration #   NI-25463 (815-13C00112) Reference Number (815-00782174)

Respected Sir,
It is in reference to Mr. Wilson s/o William for file re-opening and some important issues about them. I Most Reverend Joseph F.S. Coutts Archbishop of Karachi want to inform you that I know personally each and everything about their case and the incidence happened to them. Even the troubles they have been facing from past many years in Bangkok. I like to inform you that this family is a real victim.

The incidence started from the elder brother of Wilson William when some Muslim Mullahs came to their house with weapons and blamed their brother (Younus William) for dis-respecting Quran but later. And on their way back those Mullahs threatened them by saying that they will come back with police and will punish. After so many difficulties Mr. Younus their elder brother arrived in Thailand in 2011 and the rest of the family moved and hid themselves to different places; but then in Aug 2012 another incidence took place in which Nasreen Wilson (wife of Wilson William); while she working in Zia-Ud-Din hospital a Muslim Mullah came to the hospital with his old father during Ramdan (fasting period) and that Muslim Mullah blamed Wilson's wife for breaking his father' fast purposely and after that the family of Wilson hid them self completely.

After that incident another incident took place while the niece of the same family by the name of Sania Salamat, was going to the Church with her mother and Muslim Mullah stopped her and asked about her auntie (Nasreen Wilson) when she refused to tell him, he forcefully tried to kidnap her. But with the help of the people around, she was able to escape. Muslim people are still searching for them everywhere; they had also issued fatwa on them in which they said that wherever anyone found this family has to kill them.

Archbishop's House • St. Patrick's Cathedral • Saddar • Karachi - 74400 • Pakistan

Letter from Archbishop Joseph Coutts of Karachi regarding attacks against members of Wilson's family and their subsequent denial of refugee status by the UNHCR (continued on next page)

Catholic Archdiocese of Karachi

Later the second daughter of the same family (Nasreen Liaquat) who was staying in separate place far away from them was searched by Muslim Mullah's and these Muslim Mullah's burnt their two daughters when they were alone at home. From March 2014 parents of these two girls (who were burnt) are missing in Pakistan and still there is no news about them whether they are alive or not. The names of these two girls are Sonam Liaquat and Urisha Liaquat NT UNHCR NO. 815-14c 00355 and are still under UNHCR and have been waiting for their appeal result.

After facing lots of sufferings and troubles in Pakistan this family was rejected by UNHCR which is very shocking and disappointing news for me. I personally knows everything about them, from my sources I still have a news that those Mullah's are still searching for them. It is my humble request to you to please consider this case as this family is a real victim and need a safe life.

Thanking you and God Bless you.

+ Joseph Coutts

+ Joseph Coutts
Archbishop of Karachi

Chalk and Wilson families at Holy Redeemer Catholic Church, Bangkok

Casey Chalk with members of Wilson's family. From bottom left, clockwise: Casey Chalk; Wilson's mother, Gulzar Bibi; Wilson's father, William; family friend Naomi Patras; Wilson's wife, Maryam; and Wilson.

Appendix B

Written Testimony of Ann Buwalda
Executive Director, Jubilee Campaign USA

Submitted to the House Foreign Affairs Subcommittee on Africa, Global Health, Global Human Rights, and International Organizations for the Hearing Record on "A Global Crisis: Refugees, Migrants and Asylum Seekers"

February 26, 2019

I would like to thank Chairwoman Bass, Ranking Member Smith, and members of the Subcommittee for providing the opportunity to address the panel and submit this statement on the crisis of religious and ethnic minority refugees and asylum seekers in Thailand and elsewhere.

The United States of America has traditionally been a beacon of hope for the oppressed and persecuted suffering around the world. Ronald Reagan stated at the end of his 1980 acceptance speech as the Republican Party presidential candidate, "Can we doubt that only a divine Providence placed this land, this island of freedom, here as a refuge for all those people in the world who yearn to breathe freely: Jews and Christians enduring persecution behind the Iron Curtain, the boat people of Southeast Asia, of Cuba and of Haiti, the victims of drought and famine in Africa, the freedom fighters of Afghanistan and our own countrymen held in savage captivity?" The founding of my organization's branch in the United Kingdom stems back to the Siberian Seven refugees who gained their freedom from religious oppression in the Soviet Union through the efforts of President Ronald Reagan and who were welcomed to the United States as a result of his leadership. We are again at a cross roads of history requiring leadership where our traditional values as a welcoming nation to those suffering oppression and persecution, especially those fleeing religious based persecution, is in debate and doubt. It is my sincere hope that today's hearing will contribute to renewing the calling that the divine Providence has placed on this land.

Jubilee Campaign seeks to draw the Subcommittee's attention to the need to protect and aid religious minority refugees. Under both international refugee law and domestic asylum law, one of the five grounds of protection is a well-founded fear of persecution on account of one's religion, which includes the right to choose a belief and practice as well as maintain one's religious beliefs or none at all and the right to perform one's religious practices. At times religious refugees have been placed behind other types of refugees. Indeed, one of the reasons many of us pursued the International Religious Freedom Act of 1998 was to ensure that sufficient training and attention is placed by refugee and asylum adjudicators on religious based claims seeking refugee protection. The International Religious Freedom Act of 1998, 22 U.S.C. §§ 6401 et seq., was a response to increased religious persecution around the globe. It establishes the infrastructure for advancing religious freedom as American foreign policy and for protecting individuals who are being persecuted because of their religion. Several of its provisions address religious persecution and should be applied in giving consideration to refugee resettlement to the United States.

My testimony seeks to expose the circumstances in Thailand pertaining to a vulnerable refugee population—those seeking asylum from Pakistan. Verifiable statistics are difficult to obtain, but we currently estimate that there are 3,000 to 4,000 Pakistani Christians in Thailand who have fled religious persecution and whose cases are pending, approved and awaiting resettlement, or closed affording them with no place to go. Despite the widespread and serious persecution of religious minorities in Pakistan, a significant number of applicants in recent years are being unfairly denied refugee status by the United Nations High Commissioner for Refugees (UNHCR). More about that below, but first some context. Within a host country and based on its agreements with a host country, the UNHCR performs a critical role in protecting asylum seekers and processing refugee claims. In Thailand, the UNHCR has attempted to adhere to its commitments to asylum seekers who have swelled in numbers on account of increasing persecution in home countries. At the same time the UNHCR needs to placate the Thai government's limitations on its ability to protect asylum seekers, provide assistance, and properly adjudicate claims.

We understand from anecdotal information because exact statistics are not released by the UNHCR that in the past couple of years approximately 50 percent of Pakistani religious minority applicants are being granted refugee status by the Bangkok UNHCR office. However, this statistic is misleading, as information we have collected shows that upwards of 90 percent of cases from the Pakistani Ahmadiyya community are granted, leaving the percentage of granted Pakistani Christian cases between 10 percent and 30 percent. We find this to be disturbingly low, given the pattern of persecution of the Christian minority in Pakistan. This year the U.S. Department of State under the IRF Act of 1998 placed Pakistan "on a Special Watch List for severe violations of religious freedom." In its 2018 report the US Commission on International Religious Freedom (USCIRF) recommended Pakistan for Country of Particular Concern designation under the IRF Act. In light of these findings and so many other human rights reports, all religious minorities from Pakistan should be afforded the same burden of proof and that burden of proof should be reflective of the recognized severe violations of religious freedom experienced by these minorities in Pakistan.

Despite the severity of country conditions, the UNHCR in Bangkok unreasonably denies cases. There have been several reasons for the denials, many of which seem to be unjust. One reason appears to have been the rush to adjudicate cases during a period of extreme backlogs during 2016–2017. The backlogs at the UNHCR in Bangkok seem to have improved but potentially at the cost of denying legitimate refugee claims, and I provide below specific examples of cases we have assisted to seek reopenings and reversals of the rejections. Other organizations also active in assisting the vulnerable Pakistani Christian refugee population such as Christian Freedom International have many examples of cases we believe to be legitimate but whose claims were rejected. Some of these denials appear to be based on general skepticism as to threats faced by Christians in Pakistan, or a lack of knowledge of country conditions. There further seems to be a minimization of persecution by non-state actors, even when it appears clear that their actions either represent the positions of local law enforcement officials or are in any case unopposed by them. Another shortcoming we have observed is a perception of bias causing the UNHCR contracted interpreters to inaccurately interpret the interviews of Christian asylum seekers. This may have impacted the case of Michael D'Souza described below. Most disturbing, however, has been the imposition by the UNHCR of an unreasonable credibility test and significantly higher burden of proof as well as standard of perfection imposed on the Pakistani Christian asylum seekers. The adverse credibility findings declared in many of the decisions end up damning those Pakistani Christians, even though their claim is legitimate. I describe below the glaring example in the adjudication of Talib Masih's claim.

Jubilee Campaign has attempted to assist some of the denied cases in their appeal process with the UNHCR which have resulted in re-openings and approvals. However, those approved now have no country to which they can be referred for resettlement leaving them stuck and vulnerable in Thailand. The conditions for refugees in Thailand have been extensively detailed by Amnesty International (AI), and these findings confirm our organization's observations. The 2017 AI report notes that refugees in Thailand face many difficulties due to their lack of legal status, including "limited employment prospects, trouble accessing medical care and educational opportunities, financial stresses, self-imposed restrictions on movement and social interactions, and the constant fear of arrest. Refugees and asylum-seekers arrested for immigration violations may face prolonged and indefinite detention in appalling conditions in IDCs.... UN human rights bodies, UNHCR and civil society organizations have repeatedly raised concerns about the prolonged detention of refugees and asylum-seekers, the poor conditions in IDCs, and the impact of these factors on the physical, psychological and social wellbeing of those seeking protection in Thailand.... *Given the stark realities of detention and refugee life in Thailand, some refugees and asylum-seekers make the difficult decision to return to their home countries and face the dangers and hardships that caused them to seek protection abroad."*

This is where the other shoe drops for these refugees; whether they have been denied refugee status or are subjected to prolonged waiting for a resolution to their case, the deplorable conditions of the Immigration Detention Center (IDC) and the refugees' lack of domestic legal status leaves them hopeless, with little choice but to return to the dire circumstances they once fled from. We must emphasize the fact that people die in the IDC because they are not given access to medical treatment or are unable to pay for their medical care, medicine, or proper food.

D'Souza

Such was the situation for Michael D'Souza, a Pakistani Christian who fled to Thailand with his family in 2012. Mr. D'Souza and his family had been verbally harassed and threatened with bodily harm because of their Christian faith by various groups of Pakistani men and mullahs since 2005. Mr. D'Souza endured numerous beatings including one in which his persecutors threatened to "hang him like Jesus," as they stretched his arms out to the side and kicked his back. In 2012, two of Mr. D'Souza's sisters-in-law were kidnapped and a group of men beat Mr. D'Souza unconscious outside his home. After seeing a poster on a mosque wall with his photograph and a charge of blasphemy, Mr. D'Souza followed the advice of his friends and took his family out of Pakistan for their safety.

The D'Souzas arrived in Bangkok, Thailand, in November 2012. Mr. D'Souza received his asylum seeker certificate in December but later that month was arrested and the D'Souzas had to spend a day in the Immigration Detention Center (IDC). After paying 50,000 Thai baht, they were released. Mr. D'Souza's

Refugee Status Determination (RSD) interview was held on October 9, 2013. While waiting for a determination, the D'Souzas were arrested again and spent three weeks in the IDC. After paying bail, they were released. Mr. D'Souza's UN refugee application was rejected in 2015, and Mr. D'Souza has provided to us several examples of where his interpreter mistranslated. A subsequent appeal was denied in 2016, and the D'Souzas were again placed in IDC. After a year in IDC in difficult circumstances and with no place to go, the D'Souzas made the painful decision to self-deport to Pakistan in hopes of better things. But that was not to be.

Returning to Pakistan, Mr. D'Souza was unable to find a job, so with money from church friends in Bangkok, he bought a motorized rickshaw (tuk-tuk) to work as a taxi driver. Two months later, he was recognized by a group of men who told him that they were members of the Taliban and that they had been looking for him for years. They severely beat him with a cane and burned his tuk-tuk. Mr. D'Souza cannot work, his children cannot go to school, and he now lives in constant fear for his safety and that of his family. Sadly, Mr. D'Souza's return to Pakistan confirmed the reasons why he should have been granted his refugee status determination by the UNHCR, those whom he feared, found and bludgeoned him just as they had threatened to do years earlier.

Although refugees may appear to "voluntarily" self-deport, serious questions arise as to whether those deportations are truly "voluntary" or, due to the overwhelming economic, emotional, and physical difficulties for refugees in Thailand, whether the refugees are insidiously, indirectly coerced to deport. The AI report states, "refoulement [forceable deportment] need not be accomplished using physical coercion." International law also prohibits "constructive" refoulement, which occurs when states use indirect means to coerce the return of individuals to situations where they are likely to face human rights violations. UNHCR's "Handbook on Voluntary Repatriation" states, "The principle of voluntariness is the cornerstone of international protection with respect to the return of refugees." While a number of factors, including the economic, social and cultural pressures may affect whether a return is voluntary, lack of legal status and indefinite confinement can be chief drivers in an involuntary decision to return to one's country of origin.

For good reason, the Human Rights Watch Organization (HRW) this past November, sent a formal letter to the Prime Minister of Thailand strongly requesting that Pakistani asylum seekers in Thailand *not be sent back to Pakistan*. Most of these asylum seekers come from the Christian and Ahmadiyya communities in Pakistan and have been the main targets of the blasphemy law which carries with it the death penalty. Jubilee campaign joins with HRW in pointing out that while Pakistan has primary responsibility for protecting the religious rights of its communities, "*Thailand also has a legal responsibility to not return refugees to a place where their lives or liberty would be in danger*," as the above mentioned case of Michael D'Souza and the case of "James" featured in the AI report tragically illustrate.

Other cases currently languishing in Thailand include:

Sunny Gill

Sunny Gill is a well-known Christian journalist and documentary photographer from Pakistan. Through his political and religious activities, he has continuously raised the issues of Pakistan's voiceless minorities. Because of his work, Mr. Gill was physically assaulted by members of a criminal group associated with the Awami National Party (ANP) leading to his fleeing to Thailand where he applied to the UNHCR for refugee status. The UNHCR denied Mr. Gill's petition in 2016 with a second denial issued in 2017. Since his first denial, five activists matching Mr. Gill's profile disappeared in Pakistan. Similar to Mr. Gill, the activists were well-known for speaking out against the Pakistani military and religious militants and advocating for religious minority rights. Thankfully, the UNHCR granted a request that Mr. Gill's appeal be reopened, he was re-interviewed, and he has been granted refugee status more than a year ago. However, there is no country to which his approved case has yet been referred on account of the global retraction by countries accepting referred refugees from the UNHCR.

Talib Masih

Talib Masih, a Christian Pakistani, attended an Indian wedding celebration in 2009. Five days later, Talib and Mukhtar Masih were accused and beaten by a group of Muslim men who alleged that Mukhtar had torn pages from the Koran, burned them, and humiliated the Prophet in a pre-wedding ceremony. Local Muslim clerics accused Talib and Mukhtar of blasphemy, made inflammatory statements against the blasphemy-accused, and incited Muslim residents who destroyed the homes and business of Christians in Korian village, as well as the burning of two Protestant churches. Violence continued for days, spreading into the town of Gojra in Punjab Province. A mob of 3,000 Muslims was responsible for burning at least 107 houses, shooting indiscreetly and killing 8 Christians. Other Christians died from burn injuries. The violence forced villagers to flee. Talib Masih, after receiving severe threats, was forced into hiding for nearly two years before travelling to Thailand in 2012 seeking asylum. UNHCR denied Mr. Masih's application in 2014; and he was given a second notice of denial in 2016. Following a request prepared by Jubilee Campaign, the UNHCR reopened Mr. Masih's refugee status, re-interviewed him, and granted his refugee status in April 2017. However, Mr. Masih remains in hiding in Thailand with no country to which his approved refugee case has yet been referred on account of the global retraction by countries accepting referred refugees from the UNHCR.

Yasmin Saleem

Yasmin Saleem is a Pakistani Christian married to a Pakistani journalist. In 2012, her husband sought to help a 16-year-old Christian girl procure a divorce from a Muslim man, who had kidnapped her at gunpoint, forced her to convert to Islam, and forcibly married her. The girl's parents let her stay with Yasmin's family for protection. With the help of a Christian lawyer, the Muslim divorce was granted. The now ex-husband, who was in jail at the time of the divorce, became aggressive and tried to harass those who helped the girl. He threatened Yasmin by phone and text, threatening to kidnap Yasmin's daughter and do the same things he had done to this other girl. One day as Yasmin left work, she was struck by a car, dislocating her vertebrae. Later, she received a call from the ex-husband saying that next time she wouldn't be so lucky. Yasmin didn't contact the police because she believed the ex-husband would tell the police that she had kidnapped his wife and converted her from Islam. By the middle of 2012, the girl was no longer with Yasmin's family [who] thought the harassment would end, but the threats continued. She was harassed at work, resulting in her employer asking her to resign. After one particularly harrowing encounter with the gun-toting ex-husband at Yasmin's house, Yasmin fled to Thailand. Her husband remained in Pakistan to secure passports for their children, who joined Yasmin in 2013. The UNHCR rejected Yasmin's case in 2014 citing a lack of evidence, [and] denied the subsequent appeal in 2017; a second application was made which was also rejected for lack of evidence in 2018. [As of] December 2018 a third application with evidence has been filed on Yasmin's behalf. She remains in Bangkok, fearful of arrest by Thai authorities, unable to provide schooling to her children with her there, and terrified of being returned to Pakistan.

Another refugee community facing severe persecution are the Montagnards of Vietnam. USCIRF has cataloged the severity of persecution of this religious minority community. Our sources estimate that there are presently 500 Montagnard Christians in Bangkok, but the number is rising, as persecution increases for the million or so Montagnards in Vietnam. The treatment of Montagnard asylum seekers in Thailand is unique because immigration authorities separated families, including nursing children from their mothers. Although some mothers have been bailed out of the IDC, many mothers still remain detained, separated from their children. Most, if not all of these mothers have been recognized as persons of concern by [the] UNHCR. It's also sensitive for them because Vietnam has a history of extrajudicial kidnappings in Thailand, most recently in the case of a Radio Free Asia blogger. Also, note that a Memorandum to End Child Detention was recently signed between Thailand and the UN-HCR. As a result/prequel to this, bail is open for mothers and children registered with UNHCR, and Thai immigration now transfers mothers with children out of IDC and to more humane shelters. However, mothers from Vietnam remain separated from their children, and there are, in fact, still children in IDC.

We urge the United States to increase its efforts to welcome Pakistani Christians and other minority religious refugees such as the Montagnards awaiting resettlement in Thailand. A number of Christians have been granted refugee status by the UNHCR in Thailand but have yet to be resettled to another country. In the year 2018, the United States welcomed 338 refugees from Thailand pertaining to the Muslim religion. In contrast, only 101 Christian arrivals were reported. Pakistani Christians awaiting to be resettled need protection and prompt intervention from supportive countries such as the United States is needed. The refugee crisis facing religious minorities is by no means confined to Thailand.

Eritrea

The precarious political environment in Eritrea makes it of special concern. Human rights violations in Eritrea identified by the State Department include:
- Arbitrary deprivation of life;
- Disappearances;
- Torture and other cruel, inhumane, and degrading treatment by security forces, including for political and religious beliefs;
- Harsh prison and detention center conditions;
- Arbitrary arrest;
- Denial of fair public trial;
- Arbitrary or unlawful interference with privacy, family, or home;
- Restrictions on freedoms of speech and press;
- Restrictions on internet freedom, academic freedom, and cultural events;
- Restrictions on freedom of peaceful assembly, association, and religion;
- Limits on freedom of internal movement and foreign travel;

- Inability of the citizens to choose the government in free and fair elections;
- Corruption and lack of transparency;
- Restrictions on international non-governmental organizations;
- Violence against women and girls, including in military camp settings and national service positions;
- Human trafficking;
- Criminalization of same-sex sexual conduct;
- Forced labor, including forced participation in the country's national service program, routinely for periods beyond the 18-month legal obligation.

In an attempt to assume complete control of religious activities and teachings, the government only recognizes four religious denominations: Islam, Eritrean Orthodoxy, Catholicism, and Lutheranism. Church leaders are often selected by the government, while sermons and activities are regulated. Other faiths and denominations including Evangelicals, Pentecostals, and Jehovah's Witnesses are forced to meet and worship in secret, and if discovered, face severe consequences including arrest, torture, and imprisonment. It is estimated that over 1,000 people are in prison on account of their faith in Eritrea, including church leaders.

In 2018, 14,567 Eritreans fled the country to Ethiopia alone comprising slightly less than 40 percent of the total number of people seeking refuge in Ethiopia. Of particular concern is the high number of unaccompanied and separated children fleeing the impending military conscription. Eritreans aged between 15 and 40 are most likely to leave to avoid national service and in response to their perceived limited prospects within the country. Forty-four percent of refugees in Ethiopia are children and of that number 27 percent are Eritrean. The UNHCR noted that the onward movement of unaccompanied and separated children originating from Eritrea to urban centers and third countries was up substantially with up to 60 percent estimated to leave camps within a given year exposing the children to risk of smuggling, trafficking, and sexual- and gender-based violence.

Eritreans who left their country illegally fear the consequences of returning. They may face torture, prison, disappearance, and discrimination given their continuing objections to national service requirements and repressive government policies. In addition to that, Eritreans are subject to pay the diaspora tax and must sign a "letter of apology" at the Eritrean embassy prior to returning home (Human Rights Watch, 2015). While serious concerns about treatment on return have generally prevented the deportation of Eritreans, Sudan has repeatedly forced back Eritrean asylum-seekers and refugees to Eritrea, where they risk persecution (GSDRC, 2016). The UK removed 49 Eritreans between April and June 2015 (ibid). One Eritrean whom the United States removed last year was so distraught that he committed suicide during a layover on his return.

Aster Tewelde

Aster Tewelde is one such Eritrean who left her native country for fear of an indefinite conscription and the associated dangers for conscripted women of rape, forced marriage, and death. Aster fled to Yemen in a small boat dangerously crossing the Red Sea. While in Yemen, she married and had a son. In 2001, after Aster became a Christian, her boss began harassing her because of her Christian faith. She had to defend herself and eventually quit working altogether. Her son was suspended from school because he would not practice Islam and, later, beaten by his teacher due to his Christian faith. The teacher and students demanded that he become Muslim to stay in school, resulting in him being out of school for over a year. He received death threats after he had written in his notebook that Muhammad was a false prophet. In 2015, Aster's husband, died. It took 2 weeks to bury him because the local burial sites would not accept Christians. A neighbor helped for a few weeks, but she had to rely on others for food and help. Young men and boys continually mock her son because his father died and he was pressured to join ISIS, which he rebuffed because of his Christian faith. However, her son is afraid to leave his home as Muslims are looking for young men to recruit in the streets. Aster is unable to work due to restrictions on women in Yemen and she is unable to leave her home unless a male friend of her husband comes and takes her and her son to buy food. The UNHCR granted Aster and her son refugee status in 2014 and again in 2016, but the UN is currently unable to get to Sanaa, to renew her refugee documents. Aster has relatives in the U.S. and is seeking to come to the U.S. as a refugee. Despite the clear vulnerabilities of Aster in the country of Yemen, the United States is not processing refugee cases from Yemen, and there is no possibility of referral to any country for resettlement.

Speaking of Yemen, there are Yemeni converts in Egypt, Ethiopia and Chad who are in difficult circumstances. Converts from Islam to Christianity from Yemen and other countries face unique vulnerabilities. Children of converts are forced to take Islam in school; they cannot attend a Christian school as it could lead to the school being closed. Even when converts are registered with the UNHCR they still do not have the right to live as Christians in the country of refuge such as Egypt and Jordan. Even when they receive permission to leave the country (RSD) they can face difficulties with birth certificates and marriage certificates. For example, a woman born Muslim and whose documents state her religion at birth is not legally allowed to marry a non-Muslim. This issue is found mainly in Jordan and Lebanon.

Recommendations:

- The UNHCR in Thailand apply a consistent burden of proof and equally apply adjudication standards before making adverse credibility findings, as well as address perceived bias towards Pakistani Christian asylum seekers.
- The United States increase its refugee admission and adjust its refugee admission criteria to accept additional religious based refugees. The current refugee admission priorities should more intentionally incorporate religious minority refugees.

I thank you again for convening this hearing and allowing me to testify to the ongoing crisis of religious and ethnic minority refugees and asylum seekers.

Selected Bibliography

Bibi, Asia, and Anne-Isabelle Tollet. *Blasphemy, A Memoir: Sentenced to Death Over a Cup of Water*. Chicago: Chicago Review Press, 2013.

————. *Free at Last: A Cup of Water, a Death Sentence, and an Inspiring Story of One Woman's Unwavering Faith*. Savage, MN: Broadstreet Publishing, 2020.

Coll, Steve. *Ghost Wars: The Secret History of the CIA, Afghanistan, and Bin Laden, from the Soviet Invasion to September 10, 2001*. New York: Penguin Books, 2004.

Esack, Farid. *The Qur'an: A User's Guide*. Oxford: Oneworld Publications, 2005.

Esposito, John L. *Islam: The Straight Path*. 4th ed. New York: Oxford University Press, 2011.

Grim, Brian J., and Roger Finke. *The Price of Freedom Denied: Religious Persecution and Conflict in the Twenty-First Century*. Cambridge: Cambridge University Press, 2010.

Houllebecq, Michel. *Submission*. New York: Picador, 2015.

Jones, Owen Bennett. *Pakistan: Eye of the Storm*. 3rd ed. New Haven: Yale University Press, 2009.

Pinault, David. *The Crucifix on Mecca's Front Porch: A Christian's Companion to the Study of Islam*. San Francisco: Ignatius Press, 2018.

Rashid, Ahmed. *Taliban: Militant Islam, Oil and Fundamentalism in Central Asia*. 2nd ed. New Haven: Yale University Press, 2010.

Rippin, Andrew. *Muslims: Their Religious Beliefs and Practices*. 3rd ed. New York: Routledge, 2005.

Sheen, Fulton J. *The Mystical Body of Christ*. Notre Dame, IN: Ave Maria Press, 2015.

Sookhdeo, Patrick. *A Christian's Pocket Guide to Islam*. Pewsey, Wiltshire, U.K.: Isaac Publishing, 2004.

———. *Freedom to Believe: Challenging Islam's Apostasy Law*. McLean, VA: Isaac Publishing, 2009.

———. *Islam: The Challenge to the Church*. Pewsey, Wiltshire, U.K.: Isaac Publishing, 2006.

———. *A People Betrayed: The Impact of Islamization on the Christian Community in Pakistan*. Pewsey, Wiltshire, U.K.: Isaac Publishing, 2002.

Wright, Lawrence. *The Looming Tower: Al-Qaeda and the Road to 9/11*. New York: Vintage Books, 2007.

About the Author

Casey J. Chalk is a contributing editor at the *New Oxford Review*, a senior contributor for the *Federalist*, and a frequent contributor to the *American Conservative* and *Crisis Magazine*. He holds a B.A. in history and a master's in teaching from the University of Virginia, and a master's in theology from the Notre Dame Graduate School of Theology at Christendom College. He lives with his wife, Claire, and their four children in his native Northern Virginia.

Sophia Institute

Sophia Institute is a nonprofit institution that seeks to nurture the spiritual, moral, and cultural life of souls and to spread the gospel of Christ in conformity with the authentic teachings of the Roman Catholic Church.

Sophia Institute Press fulfills this mission by offering translations, reprints, and new publications that afford readers a rich source of the enduring wisdom of mankind.

Sophia Institute also operates the popular online resource CatholicExchange.com. *Catholic Exchange* provides world news from a Catholic perspective as well as daily devotionals and articles that will help readers to grow in holiness and live a life consistent with the teachings of the Church.

In 2013, Sophia Institute launched Sophia Institute for Teachers to renew and rebuild Catholic culture through service to Catholic education. With the goal of nurturing the spiritual, moral, and cultural life of souls, and an abiding respect for the role and work of teachers, we strive to provide materials and programs that are at once enlightening to the mind and ennobling to the heart; faithful and complete, as well as useful and practical.

Sophia Institute gratefully recognizes the Solidarity Association for preserving and encouraging the growth of our apostolate over the course of many years. Without their generous and timely support, this book would not be in your hands.

www.SophiaInstitute.com
www.CatholicExchange.com
www.SophiaInstituteforTeachers.org

Sophia Institute Press® is a registered trademark of Sophia Institute.
Sophia Institute is a tax-exempt institution as defined by the
Internal Revenue Code, Section 501(c)(3). Tax ID 22-2548708.